Cats

Cats

Listeners share their favourite cat stories with
Sarah Kennedy

First published 2002 by Contender Books
Contender Books is a division of
The Contender Entertainment Group
48 Margaret Street
London W1W 8SE

This edition published 2002

1 3 5 7 9 10 8 6 4 2

ISBN 1 84357 014 9

Typeset by Derek Doyle & Associates, Liverpool
Printed in the UK by Butler and Tanner Ltd

Dedicated to all the people who try to make a cat's life better, at home or abroad.

Thank you from Hector (spoilt rotten cat)

P.S. Hebe, Echo, Marbles and big fat Burman say thanks for all contributors' observations included in this book, which they think are totally distorted and are thinking of suing!

Foreword

The Animal Health Trust focuses on the health and welfare of companion animals, ie cats, dogs and horses. The recent increase in cat ownership has made them the most popular pet in the UK, and it is inevitable, therefore, that the number of referrals to the Trust will increase correspondingly.

To meet this demand, the Trust is establishing a new Feline Unit which will be equipped to diagnose and treat very specific conditions suffered by the domestic cat population. These will include the capacity to administer radio-iodine therapy to cats with hyperthyroidism. Although this is very common in cats, there are only four centres in the UK with the ability to give this treatment.

The Trust's fundraising programme is constantly stretched by the continual need to provide state-of-the-art equipment, facilities and expertise. The generosity of our supporters such as Sarah Kennedy, who is donating the royalties from this book to the Feline Unit, is vital. Without such initiatives, the Trust simply could not continue to operate at the leading edge of veterinary science.

We are extremely grateful to Sarah, not only for her support in this way but for her ongoing interest in our work.

Ted Chandler BVetMed, FRCVS
Executive Chairman
AHT

Introduction

There are now nine million cat owners in this country — that's put a few dog owners' noses out of joint — grrr! Yes, cats overtook dogs as our most popular faithful friends several years ago. I can come clean and admit to being brought up with goldfish, two donkeys, numerous puppies, a brace of budgies and a Siamese. The puppies always got trapped in deck chairs; the donkeys took a dislike to my aunt and took a chunk out of her bottom on one Christmas walk; the budgies messed up Mother's new machine-sewn curtains; I flushed the goldfish down the loo while washing the bowl (I was heartbroken — goldfish wasn't too pleased, either); but the Siamese? Wonky was so named because of his kinky tail, and legend has it that Cleopatra hung her jewels on their tails, hence the kink.

One Christmas Eve, the aforementioned Siamese sneaked into the larder and devoured half the turkey. Never fazed, Mother sewed it all up (being a nurse) and muttered the immortal words: 'Your father will never notice.' If he did notice that the bird was on a tilt and only had one leg, he tactfully never said anything, but I noticed he had an appointment with the optician on 27th December!

Having filmed for 12 years with Dr Desmond Morris, we had the delight of visiting the homes of devoted pedigree cat breeders. Mainly women, their menfolk patiently erected large pens and lost their vegetable patches to their wives' passion for their particular breed. These cat breeders would rise at dawn to travel to cat shows, their living rooms were decorated with rosettes and we found all cat ladies to be very hospitable and they baked wonderful biscuits and chocolate cakes for the film crews. Could they have been bribing us to show their little darlings at their best? Have you ever tried filming cats? It's as if they *know* they are having their picture taken, so immediate action is required. Having sat quietly looking beautiful for an hour, out comes the Box Brownie and they turn and show you half their backside! Mark my words, cats *know*!

This brings me to Hector, the inspiration for this mini-tome. Echo, his mother, is a complete strumpet and it had been impossible to have her spayed because she was still feeding kittens, but also going out to 'play'. The result was two small tabbies and one little white, the latter of which we kept. Our Radio 2 Dawn Patrol listeners rallied to the call. We needed a name with Greek connections to add to Marbles (as in Elgin), Hebe (named after the young Athenian warriors and also meaning 'youthful beauty' in Greek) and Echo (as in Narcissus). Oedipuss, Zeus — listeners kept 'em coming — but Hector seemed to suit him, so Hector he became, named after the son of King Priam of Troy, assassinated by Achilles. Listeners also added the stories behind *their* cats' names: 'We bought him from a psychiatrist, so called him Freud, but he's now Egg — Freud Egg'; keep up! Listeners also included weird and wonderful cat ways: how did that hot half leg of lamb get through the cat flap?...

Hector has turned into a very large white cat with a huge long white ruff and topaz eyes. When he's older I'll show him the book, which he'll probably eat. Ah well, he's destroyed all the furniture but we still love them, don't we? I just wish he'd curb his habit of tunnelling under the rugs. He'd have been an asset in Colditz trickling sand down his legs! I do hope you enjoy the book and read about the Animal Health Trust, which is starting up a new feline division whose research will go into feline disease prevention. It's a very good project and I've been there to see their work for myself.

In the meantime, remember that however many hunting trophies he deposits on the Axminster; however many plant pots she knocks off the window sill; and however much food they take when your back is turned — cats are still one of the best companions you could ever have!

Sarah Kennedy

Inspirational Names for Cats

Tourist attraction

When we moved into our house 14 years ago, we were given a house-warming present of an eight-week-old bundle of fluffy Persian kitten. We later discovered that he was born on the very day we moved in.

None of the classical and Persian heroic names from Agamemnon through to Xerxes seemed quite right so, since his main occupation was sleeping, we called him Mogadon (after the sleeping pill), which also shortens conveniently to 'Mog'. Over the years, he has been a much-loved and well-known feature of Hastings Old Town as he sits outside our front door on the sea front, which is passed by hundreds of visitors and locals every day. He has recently lost an eye, which he doesn't seem to mind – in fact, his visual celebrity has rather been enhanced by his Cyclops-like appearance!

Annie and George Greaves

Cat or milkman?

Our cat is called Diesel, as he has a very loud purr which sounds like the diesel engine of the milk lorry that comes up our road every day.

Clive and Eve Fisher

Fancy a beer?

My friends next door had two cats called Cefor, as in C for cat and Widget, as in the little gadget at the bottom of beer cans that makes the beer become very lively when opened by the ring-pull. At the time widgets featured prominently in beer adverts on TV, and the dictionary definition is: 'Any small mechanism or device, the name of which is unknown or temporarily forgotten', which suited the cat very well.

Marjorie Ward

Not in front of the neighbours!

Richard once had a cat who had a kink right at the end of his tail and was therefore called Kinky. Calling him in late at night always produced twitching curtains!

Yvonne and Richard Crowther

Logical thinking?

I work as a tanker driver delivering chemicals throughout the UK, and one of the sites I visit is called ICI Rocksavage, commonly known as Rocky. They have quite a collection of feral cats, which are fed by ICI personnel and drivers alike. One particular day one of the loaders asked me if I wanted a kitten, but as I already have a dog I said no. I had a look anyway, and when I saw this little ball of shivering wet fur under a bush I cleaned it up and put it in my cab. Just as we caught it, another one ran along the wall, so we caught that one as well. I took them both home, much to the displeasure of my wife, with the intention of taking them to a cat rescue centre. But nobody wanted the cats and the following night I caught my wife at 3 a.m. on her hands and knees feeding them. I said we should call one of them Rocky, as they were found at ICI Rocksavage (we ended up calling her Roxy as she was female) and my wife said we should call the other one Lily, as in Lily Savage!

Paul Dunwoody

Oops!

Some years ago we got a cat from a local cat rescue centre. She was a lovely three-year-old jet black beast called Tammy, who had already been spayed, which we were pleased about. After a few days, we took Tammy to the vet for a check-up. After about 10 seconds, our bemused vet informed us that 'Tammy' was at least eight years old, unneutered and male! In the end we called him Kiwi, because he was 'all black'.

Sharon

Cat or car?

When I lived at my previous house there was a stray cat down the road with only three legs. Everybody affectionately called him Robin (as in Reliant).

Jackie Marshall

Cat or car again!

It was November 1985 and it had snowed heavily, followed by rain, which made it very slushy. It was late evening and time to take our 17-year-old dog George for his walk. When I let George off his lead so he could head for the fields, I heard a very demanding miaow. As it was so dark, I couldn't see where it was coming from at first. I stood by one of the many parked cars that lined the kerb, when I caught a pair of eyes looking at me from behind the front wheel of the car next to me. I got down to have a look and found a soaking wet, bedraggled kitten, still miaowing demandingly. I fished her out, called George and rushed home to dry her off and warm her up. She stayed on our best armchair, asleep, for two whole days, waking only to eat and answer the call of nature. We decided to keep her, as two weeks later George died, but we didn't know what to call her. I remembered the car she was under when I found her, and decided to call her Mini. She is still demanding and still hogs the best chair.

G. Davies

Cat or camel?

Back in the 1970s we had a lovely black and white kitten for the children, but what to call her? After much deliberation, we decided on Twiggy. When she was a bit older, we took her to the vet to be 'done'. He took one look and said, 'You have a two-brick job here – it won't cost you half as much!' In our innocence, we asked him what he meant and he told us the joke about the chap who took a camel to be castrated. The vet did the job by clapping two house bricks together! 'Ouch!' said the owner. 'Doesn't that hurt?' The vet replied, 'Yes, it does a bit. I should have used gauntlets!' So Twiggy became Wiggy after that and we had to relate the camel joke many times over.

Ron and Rosemary Grinsted

It's all Greek to me

Molly, my tom-cat, was the first thing I acquired at the age of 18 the week I left home. I had no money and no furniture, but when I saw 'kitten free to good home' in the local paper, I had to have it. The owners told me he was a girl, hence the name. I have spent the last 12 years shouting at people who seem to find it difficult to call a boy by a girl's name. My husband, who is obsessed by all things Greek, has called his cat Thersites (a Greek soldier, apparently) and we acquired a homeless cat, named Athena. I won the battle in naming our daughter, Demelza – she narrowly escaped the moniker 'Aphrodite'!

Rebecca Palmer

A toyboy for me!

After I got divorced, I became tired of people asking about my love life and when I might get married again. So I got myself a little kitten and called him 'Toyboy'. Thereafter, when asked the perennial question, I could quite simply answer by saying, 'I've got myself a toyboy.' This seemed to keep them quiet! Toyboy is now 10 years old and I have been happily married to Jim for six years. We often wonder how many other cats have the same name.

Caroline Bowers

Computer cats

My cats are called Gizmo, Buttons and Widget. Gizmo (a.k.a. Gizzie or Fat Slug) was abandoned and got his name from the Gremlin and because I work with computers, which were classified as gizmos by the rest of the family. Buttons (a.k.a. Butsy or Psycho-buts) is so-named because her big green eyes stand out like buttons on her black fur, and because there are buttons on keyboards. Widget (a.k.a. Wiggley-git or Widgey-woo) is so-called because it means just another gadget really. We could have called her 'Mouse', but we didn't want a cat with a split personality!

Angie Bradley

Supermarket cats

As a rescue organisation, we often get frantic calls from the public. One such call came from the manager of the local branch of Sainsburys. A Siamese cat had been found in a cat box amongst the rubbish bins at the store. Naturally, we called him Sainsbury. Then a couple brought in a large black cat who had been living rough in the local Tesco car park. He scrounged food from the customers as they loaded their cars and this couple had been making special purchases for him throughout the summer, but decided he needed to be safe and warm before winter set in. Needless to say, we called him Tesco. Both were successfully re-homed.

'Handsome' came to us as the scraggiest, ugliest Persian you have ever seen, his coat totally matted and covered in diesel oil. After treatment, he recovered. Another stray brought in was 'Tishoo', who had dreadful 'flu and sadly didn't make it. We experience both joy and sadness on a daily basis at the sanctuary, but never boredom.

Cindy Waldron, Nine Lives Sanctuary

Aptly named

My own favourite cat names are: Keith Prowse, named after the theatre ticket booking agency, as most cats tend to occupy the best seat in the house; Pavarotti, only suitable for the large cat with the voice to match; Oliver, as per the Charles Dickens character, because so many hungry cats are forced into a life of petty theft to survive; and Itchy and Scratchy for those prone to the odd flea.

During my college days, we had a caretaker whose cat we nicknamed 'Fire', as we only ever used to see the caretaker putting the cat out. Can you imagine, though, shouting, 'Fire!' on the doorstep every night to call him in?

Anonymous

Silly name?

A few years ago my parents acquired a new kitten and there was much debate about naming the very cute little ginger tom. Being the bossiest in the family, I usually have the final say, and in the past we'd had Pixie, Primrose, Lucy and Linus, and since leaving home I'd had my tortoiseshell Alice. My little sister Paula said as she was living at home, she would name the cat and he wasn't going to have a silly name like Alice – he would be called ... Keith! She was very hurt when we all laughed.

Lesley Weeks

Freudian slip?

When I was a child my mother acquired a Siamese kitten from a psychologist. She wanted to name it after a prominent psychologist, but we children had each already chosen a name for it. A compromise was reached and Mum decided to use all the names, so he was called Sigmund Sebastian Henry Percival Freud. Upon hearing this name, my Dad added the word egg – and guess which name stuck? Yes, our cat was called Freud Egg to the end of his days.

Jo Pilling

Posh cat

When I was a lad we were adopted by an old stray silver tabby, an enormous semi-feral cat that just turned up one day and never left. Our neighbours thought he looked very aristocratic, but had obviously fallen upon hard times. He was afraid of nobody and would take on any other cat, even once a passing Alsatian dog. Occasionally, I had to climb a tree to escape his frenzy, but he was a much-loved companion throughout my childhood. The only animal ever to get the better of him was a grey squirrel, which bit right through the base of his tail. He therefore became known as Sir Claude Bottom of Petts Wood.

Nigel Hammond

7

From dog to cat

Having owned Jack Russell terriers for nearly 30 years, cats had never been on our agenda. We lost our last dog just over a year ago and decided to have a break from pets for a while. However, we started catching glimpses of a large, very wild tabby cat that was obviously living rough. After the demise of our last dog, we noticed paw marks on the bonnet of the car in the garage and, as the weather was cold, we thought we would help a lost soul out, and left food in the garage for it every night. This went on for five months. Occasionally we saw the tabby cat, but as soon as he saw us he was off like a shot – so we christened him Wyatt, as in Wyatt Earp the cowboy, the fastest thing in the West! In March our back door was open and, to our great surprise, the cat walked in, had a look around, liked what he saw and has been with us ever since.

Penny Cartwright

Long line of cats

As an ardent cat lover, I've owned many over the years. First there was Ming, so named for three reasons: he had a large black M shape on his tabby forehead, my love of anything oriental, and my Dad's passion for Flash Gordon, Ming being one of the characters. Next came Cheng, named after a river in China that I discovered in my old school atlas. He was really too young to leave his mother and was so small that I used to carry him around in my apron pocket, mainly to stop him from getting stuck behind the cooker and for fear of treading on him. A while before Cheng died, we got ChooChoo, a kitten who would have been put to sleep if we hadn't had him. He was all black and named by my son, who was an avid watcher of the cartoon, *Top Cat*. ChooChoo used to curl up with the elderly, arthritic Cheng licking and grooming him, and making his last few months a pleasure. A couple of years before ChooChoo died, Sam appeared on our porch, a tiny white and tabby scrap. The vet told us 'he' was in fact a 'she', so she became Samantha.

The next feline resident was Ben, named after Benson in the American TV programme and the present incumbent is Henry, whose name just happened. He is marmalade and white and adored by all, especially my grandchildren.

Patricia Stevens

Cat cabaret

I got my cat from a cat shelter, where she had already been named by the vets. She is tortoiseshell striped and is called Moulin. Her brother, who was in the next cage, all black with lovely green eyes, was called Rouge.

Evelyn Hughes

Jazzy cats

I love cats and listening to jazz music, so it seemed only right to name my two Basie and Ellington (as in Count and Duke).

Linda Humphries

Float like a butterfly, sting like a bee

I was researching my family tree and found my great-great-Grandmother and said, 'Ah, there you are Mary Ann Puddephut,' and a little voice said, 'Miaow!' I looked down to see a fat, little black cat staring up at me. 'Is that your name?' I asked. Once again, she said, 'Miaow!' so Puddephut she became.

However, a fortnight later we came downstairs to find a thin, little black cat and five kittens. I commented that they were a bunch of heavyweights, so they became: Cassius (Clay), Rocky (Marciano), Sonny (Liston), Smokin' Joe (Frazier), and Tyson (Mike).

Jacqueline

Something in the air

My late husband's cousin, who lives in Fleetwood, has a cat called Ozone because he is very friendly!

Eve Twentyman

Cat-alogue of names

I'm a marmalade cat called Robertson and my friend next door is called Octopussy, because he's the eighth cat the family has had. I also know a Persian blue, rather a snob, called Gainsborough (famous for his portrait, *The Blue Boy*). Down the road are Muffin and Mittens – one has a white muff around his neck and Mittens has white paws. One other cat I know is called Astrophe and there's a sleek, black tom in the flats in the next road called Pushkin.

Robertson

Itchy and Scratchy

I once had a ginger cat called Tigger, who adopted me just after I'd moved into my present house. She just walked into my kitchen and started making a fuss of me as if we were old friends. Shortly after this, I started to itch. I felt that Tigger was the cause, but I didn't know why. I bought some flea powder, but all that happened was that the cat's eyes went bright pink.

I then had the bright idea of giving the cat a bath, but didn't know how. I have bathed many dogs in my time, but never a cat. So, rather than get the water too hot, I had a bath first, then tried to get the cat into the same bath water. It was a big mistake – I didn't know that cats could stretch their legs out both ways, not to mention the awful noise that Tigger was making! Next, I tried to give her a bath in the kitchen sink, which worked much better, but the itching continued. In desperation, I got the

Environmental Health people in to bombard the house with flea killer, but still the itching continued. Eventually, I found out that I was allergic to cats!

Jim McGarry

SOS

We had some friends with a cat called Help. As you can imagine, they didn't call him in at night!

Audrey Irvine

Lethal weapon!

We took over the care of a hitherto anonymous moggie when a neighbour moved. The name problem was solved one day when he was seen delivering a hefty left hook to a rival feline. He was thereafter known and loved as Bruno. During the time of the Gulf War, the same moggie was nicknamed, due to his propensity for homing in on targets swiftly and silently, under cover of darkness – the Scud!

Mary Strutt

Potty about bells!

I once had a cat I called Potto, after a haulage company based in the north, called Prestons of Potto. I was born in Preston and loved the name Potto, so that's what he had to be. I still travel up the A1 and see these lorries, and it always makes me smile. My other cat I called Bella. I found her as a kitten by a church and the bell was chiming the time.

Margaret Haines

Football crazy

I have 12 cats and they are all named after Leicester City players (some are ex-players). They are: Pegguy, Stanley Collymore, Zagorakis, Flowers, Royce, Izzet, Robbie, Muzzy, Impey, Hissinghil, Theo and Zago (kittens of Zagorakis). As you have guessed, we are footie mad!

Moira Baker

Clever cat?

A few years ago a neighbour of mine stood yelling, 'Marmite! Marmite!' for her black and white cat. At the same time, I had two cats called Muffin and Moomin. My friend and her daughter call their cats Ragga and Muffin, and many years ago my brother used to have a cat named, ironically, Mastermind. He spent ages making a cat flap in the back door, but Mastermind couldn't get used to it and would sit waiting for someone to open it for him!

Janice Clough

Compost kitty

I found my kitten, whose mother was a feral cat, on the compost heap. He was a lovely black and white male. I rescued him and called him Compo.

Helen Walker

Oily cat

We once had a kitten from a Bonnington Farm, so we called her Bonnie. My younger son Peter, then aged two, decided to see what she looked like immersed in a bucket of sump oil! She survived and was known for the rest of her life as Bonnieolly.

Sheila Hodgson

Puss-in-pants!

We thought you might find our Blue Persian's name – P.V. – quite amusing. When we bought her, we decided her pedigree name was too fancy, so plumped for the name Blue Belle. However, the journey from the breeder's place to her new home proved too much for her, and a terrible gastronomic incident resulted in a severe case of 'pantalon vert'! Hence, the name P.V.

Michael and Georgina Lewis

Him or her?

My mother had cats before I was born (I'm now 25) so there have been many entertaining names over the years. One of my favourites was Dasher, a female tortoiseshell who could warp the space-time continuum by going from A to C without passing through B! Another one was Prim (short for Prim and Proper), a rather cute long-haired tabby who walked in one day brandishing her fluffy tail and singing in her sweet voice. She was sent to the vet to be neutered, but it wasn't until after the vet had put Prim to sleep, shaved her and opened her up that he discovered that she wasn't Mrs Prim, but Mr! Other cats we have owned include Tooty (all black except for two white toes), Bonge (a ginger cat), Samantha Grey (a female grey, funnily enough) and Whitey (yes, a white cat!)

Phil Sharpe

Plan(gent)?

My partner, Fenella Gent, names her cats to fit with her surname, hence: Dili(gent), Tan(gent) and Exi(gent). The exception was a very laid-back cat she named Yoh!

Philip Holmes

Wanton cats

Some years ago I acquired a beautiful, female Burmese kitten. Believing that cats have names which are destined to be theirs, I just couldn't find the right one for her until one day when an ex-boyfriend came round trying to get into my good books. The cat was behaving rather amorously, so her name from then on was Trollop. I was never allowed to have kittens as a child, so I let Trollop have one litter of kittens – two girls and a boy. Their names could only be Crumpet, Strumpet and Humphrey (just because the name was made for him) and they all lived to a great age.

Shelley Dawson

Famous cats

My cat Daisy Bazoon is named after a character in a film (Bazoon in *The Devil's Advocate*). My kitten Rosie's name was inspired by a song by the band AC/DC called 'Whole Lotta Rosie'!

Jo-Anne Tranter

Likely cats

My cat Buddy originally belonged to a lifelong friend of mine who sadly died – so the cat became Buddy, as in friend. Maisie looks distinctly like Maisie Moscow, the novelist, whose book *Almonds and Raisins* I was reading at the time; and José is long, thin and black with large dark Spanish eyes, so what was more apt than that!

Edna Hulme

In the navy

For many years my parents, Hilda and Maurice, had a family cat named Sippers. The name is based on an old navy tradition, as my father was in the Royal Navy throughout the Second World War years. When each man was issued with his daily ration, if he owed a debt or favour, or just as a token of regard or friend-ship to his colleague, he would give part of his rum ration to the person to whom he owed the debt or favour. He would say 'sippers', 'gulpers', or 'sandy bottoms', depending on how deep he was in debt! Our cat Sippers lived to the grand old age of 21 and enjoyed every moment of her long life.

Tony Naylor

Life in the fast lane!

Our cat is called Fastlane, because that is where I rescued her from as a six-week-old kitten, in the Cardiff evening rush hour with traffic thundering by, more than 16 years ago. I put her in the car and she promptly hid in the box section under the front seats from where, after about half an hour of fishing around, my wife Nella eventually pulled her, hands dripping with blood. Fastlane is not as violent these days, but she has never stopped devising new ways to annoy us over the years. Her latest, after having used the litter tray perfectly well her whole life, is to stand in the tray and pee on the floor!

Ian Statham

Standing on ceremony

About 15 years ago we visited a vineyard in Sussex and our host was a very entertaining chap. In the car park was a lovely little kitten who was hiding under the cars and darting about, producing lots of 'aahs' from the visitors, including ourselves. We asked what the cat's name was and our host replied, 'Oh, that's Ceremony.' Seeing our puzzled looks, he explained, 'That's because he's always getting under our feet and we keep standing on him!'

Julie Dines

Going nuts

We had a wonderful ginger tom-cat who was named Gingernut until he had his 'operation' – and then he was called Ginger.

Janet Webster

Greedy cat

Some time ago, my wife was making pasta and had hung it up to dry. We had to go out for a while, and when we returned we found that half of it was missing. No prizes for guessing where the missing half had gone, considering that our cat was only a year old at the time. We ended up with a fat, furry little balloon with four little leggies sticking out as the pasta fermented inside him!

Chris Hayward

Turbo-charged

We have two cats: Topsy, who is old, fluffy, soft and cuddly; and Turbo, who is two and aptly named. When he was tiny, he thought he was a dog because he had a favourite bright pink foam ball that he would fetch and bring for us to throw! He is a good mouser, but he never brings any into the house. We have a computerised cat flap so he has to put the mouse down in order to activate the flap, which of course closes when he turns around to pick up the mouse!

Turbo is also very sociable. When he was first allowed out, we had numerous phone calls alerting us to his whereabouts: the local pub, where he had curled up on a customer's lap (the customer assumed he belonged to the pub); some new neighbours, who found him asleep on their new white sofa; and some other neighbours, whose barbecue he had joined for a whole afternoon!

Val Christmas

Paw marks

I used to own a boarding cattery and was also heavily involved with cat rescue, so cat names were all-important. There are three names that spring to mind immediately. The first was Basher Hatt – he came to board and didn't do any bashing. The second was Chips Fisher, who also spent his holidays with me and loved his fish! Best of all, though, was a little kitten I rescued. He was jet black and, as I had had a surfeit of 'Blackies' and 'Sooties', I called him Inky. Eventually he was put up for adoption, and a young lady called Lisa came to see him and fell in love with him. It was only when I was filling in her details on the adoption form that I realised how very well suited these two were. My little black rascal was to become Inky Marks!

Liz Kelly

Pregnant paws

My cat Korky always used to come and sit on my lap for a cuddle when I got home from work, and purr at me while I was having a reviving cup of tea. However, when I became pregnant, he used to have a bit of trouble staying on my bump. A few weeks before my son was born, we were sitting like this enjoying each other's company, when Korky felt the most almighty kick – from the inside! I've never seen him move so fast, or look so perplexed!

Kate Daniels

Strange passenger

Pussy-Willow, half Siamese, was always seeking our company. She came for walks with the dog, yelling in protest because we walked too fast; she would sit on my shoulders while I did the gardening, purring in my ear and patting my hair for encouragement. Finally, she would sit on the dog's back, which was warm and woolly, waiting at the gate for us to return home.

Katie and David Lane

Where's that cat?

My beloved and I are from New Zealand and are employed respectively as housekeeper/cook and handyman/gardener on a very large estate with enormous house to match. One day a villager called in to enquire if we had seen his cat, which had gone missing. We hadn't, but said we would keep an eye out for it and let him know if we found his cat. We had a look around the grounds and in some empty outbuildings, in case it had inadvertently got locked in, but to no avail. The following morning when I entered the kitchen, my dearly beloved stated that he had heard the cat, either in the ceiling or under the floorboards, he wasn't quite sure, but he had definitely heard it miaowing.

As the owner of the cat had been working on a cottage next to the estate, dearly beloved wandered down there to tell him the good news. However, when he returned he was looking rather sheepish (we Kiwis are noted for that!). I completely cracked up to hear that, when he relayed his story about the missing moggie, he was asked: 'Do you listen to Sarah Kennedy on Radio 2?' Dearly beloved wasn't quite sure where the line of questioning was leading, but was horribly embarrassed when informed that the pussy-cat miaow he had heard had been played over the radio!

Carol Holden

High jump

Some friends of ours had a tabby with white bib and socks called Mr Todd. In order to save opening and shutting the kitchen door so many times, the wife persuaded her husband to fit a cat flap. This was purchased from a local DIY store and, in order to do the job properly, the husband took the door off its hinges and carried it to his workshop behind their garage.

However, when the work was completed and the door re-hung, they discovered that the cat flap was in the wrong place. All our friends had to do now was to train Mr Todd to jump five feet into the air in order to take advantage of this new device. When this proved to be impossible, they had to buy a new door and start all over again!

Mrs J Sanders

Never mind the hairdo!

14 years ago I was given two farmyard kittens who were really too young to leave their mother. They didn't know how to keep clean, so every night I had to wash them. My son Jim said that one, when wet, looked like Sid Vicious (because of the punk hairdo), so we called them Syd and Nancy, both being female. They are still with me.

Janet Hutchinson

Togetherness

My sister suffers from tinnitus quite badly and when things get a bit too much, she takes herself off to the lounge and makes herself comfortable on the carpet, with some quiet music play-ing and perfumed lavender filling the air. Imagine her surprise one afternoon when she 'came to' to see her tabby cat Tubby sprawled out on the sofa beside her, so she quietly got up and took his photograph.

Peggy Kieser

Mum's the word

My daughter was offered a kitten just at the time that she and my son were thinking of getting me a cat for Mother's Day. I had always had cats, but at that time I only had a golden retriever called Poppy. As the kittens were not ready to leave their mother, we decided to go down and choose one. I had already decided I'd like a black kitten and preferably female and when we saw them there was one that fitted the bill. At the time I was reading a book in which there was a girl called Mushka (Russian for Marie), which I really liked and, after going through several other names, decided Mushka it was to be. At the allotted time we went to pick her up – she was absolutely gorgeous, all black with blue eyes. Naturally, we booked her in with the vet to have her injections. He examined her, only to tell us that Mushka was in fact a male kitten, so we are now the proud owners of a male kitten with a girl's name. But, as the vet said, he won't realise unless we tell him.

Anne Bedford

What a handle!

Our cat is called George and sometimes we give him his full title of George Frederick Handel, on account of his musical miaow.

Susan and Alistair Le Tissier

What's going on ear?

Our last kitten, Claudia (clawed, dear) was a tortoiseshell and when she was the right age I asked my daughter to take her to the vet as we didn't want any mistakes with the local Sir Lancelot. When Lucinda went to collect her, the vet said, 'I'm afraid I've removed her ear.' 'But,' said Lucinda, 'I brought her in to have her insides removed, as we didn't want her to have kittens!' 'No,' said the vet, 'I mean she's not a Claudia – she's a Claude!'

Bebo in Devon

21

Boy or girl?

Just before Christmas one year we acquired a tiny kitten. We didn't know what sex it was, but some people looked and said, 'Oh, definitely a girl,' and others said, 'It's a boy.' Most people, like us, admitted their ignorance. At Christmas we had the usual family gathering at my house, including my daughter and young grandson. After lunch, when everyone was replete and lolling about, the kitten was on the floor at my grandson's feet, washing itself with one leg slung over its shoulder, as cats do. My grandson looked down at him and turned to his mother in alarm. 'Mum, Mum!' he cried. 'This cat's got something wrong with it – there's a spike sticking out of it!' My daughter looked down at the cat, turned to me and said, 'It's definitely a boy.' Hence, Spike got his name and is now a lovely two-year-old tabby.

Sheila Bolton

The last laugh

I used to live in Australia in the '60s and my cat was named Yabbadabbadoo, the catchphrase in the popular *Flintstones* show that was all the rage then. When I took Yabbi (as we used to call her) to the vet's one day, they asked me to fill in a form for the cat. Imagine my horror and embarrassment (along with my parents', who were there with me) when they opened the surgery door and called out, 'Yabbadabbadoo Leys, please!' We can laugh about it now.

Darlene Cavill

Bush babies

Back in 1996 we were living in a lovely old house surrounded by woodland in which lived several families of feral cats. I was catless for the first time in 25 years. I used to catch glimpses of kittens, but they could never be approached. One very cold, frosty morning I noticed a mother cat and three kittens eating the food I'd put out for the birds. Over the next few months I fed them every day. Then the mother and one of the kittens disappeared. The remaining two kittens would eat from my hand, but were still very nervous. I named them Bush (large, long-haired and black) and Rhodi (small, short-legged and tabby), as they would always appear out of a rhododendron bush. One day I noticed that the tabby was pregnant. Some time later, one chilly windy day, Rhodi came for her breakfast with a slim tummy. The whole family searched for and found five kittens not far away and very newly born. We took them in and looked after them – very time-consuming, but very enjoyable watching the five little characters develop. I named them before I knew what sex they were. They were Deni (as in rhododendron), Wistaria, Azalea, Buddleia and Camellia! After the visit to the vet, I discovered that the only girl was Deni, the little fluffy black runt. The other four were big bully-boys! Accordingly, Wistaria became Wizzy, Buddleia became Buddy, Azalea became Lear and Camellia is now known as Charlie!

Sara Pell-Stevens

Peris the peril

My wife and I like to go walking in Wales and are both particularly fond of the Snowdonia area. At the north-western end of the Llanberis Pass there is a small village called Nant Peris. We have been through the village on many occasions and at times when the sky is overcast and the rocks are wet, the place seems to exude a grey colour all of its own. Peris, being a completely grey cat, matches this colour perfectly and so the place was the inspiration for his name.

As a first-time cat owner going to collect a vehicle-battered little cat, though, I was not prepared for all the duties my wife and I would have to perform for him: feeding him mashed prawns to build up his strength (this was supposed to be for the first month, but has continued); attending to his wounds (he likes to go out in the evenings to challenge anything that moves);

carrying out minor repairs to the furniture (he likes to keep his claws in tip-top condition for fighting); roaming the streets looking for him at all hours of the day and night (he likes to watch us do this from a selection of hidden vantage points!)

Paul and Caroline Tovell

Poetry, anyone?

When we lived in Bridge of Don, we had a couple of neighbours who had two gorgeous Burmese cats, and of an evening you could hear them gently calling 'Dylan ... Thomas!' Needless to say, this caused great hilarity in the small circle where we lived.

Jill Nicoll

Ginger mischief

A pregnant cat adopted my aunt and I soon found out that I had to find a name for one of the new arrivals. My all-time wish has been to have a ginger cat, so when I found out that one of the five kittens was ginger, I knew that was the one for me. However, because I was soon off to America to study, I decided the name had to have a link with America. Therefore, he was christened Charlie Brown, in honour of the *Peanuts* cartoon. Whenever I phone home I get regular progress reports from my mum on how Charlie Brown is doing, usually punctuated by a scream or reprimand because Charlie has just entered and is causing mayhem. Letters from home also quote tales of mischief and daring undertaken by my sweet, innocent kitten. If it continues much longer, I think he will be shipped over to me because the cute little kitten in the photos on my wall never does any of the things he reportedly does at home!

Amii Etheridge

Famous five

We have five cats who very kindly let us share their bed, as long as we twist ourselves around their chosen positions. Oliver was so named because he was very greedy (as in 'Please sir, can I have some more?'). Then came E-Reg. While walking home from the pub with a ginger tom wrapped up in a Boddington's bar cloth (his claws were very sharp), we were discussing names when a brand new E-registration car went past. 'That's the first E-registered car I've seen,' I said. 'Let's call him E-Reg!' It seemed a good idea until we took him on his first visit to the vet where his name had to be called out, to much amusement. Then came Willow and Bracken, named after the flora at the farm from where we collected them (Bracken was sadly killed in an accident). Next came the dynamic duo, Friday, and her brother, Ming. Friday came pre-named, as she was born on Good Friday. We couldn't decide on a name for her brother until one day Pauline, my better half, said (with lovely spoonerism): 'I must ming my rum!' So Ming he was.

Barry and Pauline Murfett

Beatle cats

We lost our old cat Pepper at the age of 19 about six years ago. Our border collie, Sheba, had spent nine years 'herding' her and was quite devastated when she died. Sheba had to have two big operations and we promised that if she made a good recovery we would get a kitten. We ended up getting not one, but two kittens, naming them Ellie and Suki. A few weeks later I was cuddling Suki and discovered that 'she' was in fact a 'he' – so we had to have an urgent re-think on her name. A male cat with a name like Suki could give him a complex. The next thought was, what would go with Ellie? We lengthened Ellie to Eleanor and 'Rigby' came instantly to mind. He was renamed from that day and in spite of being constantly mixed up with Rigsby (of Leonard Rossiter fame in *Rising Damp*), has become a very proud and beautiful male cat.

Judie Hutchinson

Pushy puss

Just after my husband and I were married, a stray black cat popped in through the cat flap. Knowing how much trouble a stray can be when mixed with house cats, of which we already had six, we politely but firmly ejected him. The next night he was back. Again, he was told to disappear by my husband. The same thing happened for six nights. The cat would saunter into the living room, as only a cat can, as if he owned the place. He would then be thrown out again, just to prove he didn't. The final straw came when he stole a slice of pizza from my husband's plate. 'If he's going to eat my bloody food, he can eat cat food!' he spluttered. He's been with us ever since and, because he always came back after being thrown out, we called him Boomerang.

Natalie Rockett

Endless!

Our first Siamese kitten never stopped talking or purring all the way on the journey from his birth home in Norfolk to our home in Sussex. We called him Ceaseless. Then we were given a tabby. He was very sweet, but turned out to be very thick, so he became Witless. A little later a very pregnant red queen turned up on our doorstep and, as she was so small and was a very odd shape, she became Shapeless. So Ceaseless, Witless and Shapeless made up our cat family for several happy years.

When Ceaseless died, we were given another Siamese who was all grey. We called him Pointless. To continue the tradition, our next two were called Dauntless (very brave, even as a kitten) and Doubtless, who was timid to begin with, but my wife said he would doubtless become braver.

Johnny Bramall

Pink panther

We have recently had a new addition to the household. He is small and furry with a long tail, brown and grey stripes, and a cream belly covered in spots. When he first arrived he was christened with a cute name – Bailey – but after the first week, he showed his true personality and is now called Kato. This is not some male version of Kate, but he's named after the character in the *Pink Panther* films. The naughty little chap likes nothing better than to hide round corners, under beds, under clothes (particularly newly washed ones) waiting for a victim, or a victim's ankles, to be exact. When in range, he pounces, sticking his tiny, needle-like claws into anything soft. We get fed up of shouting, 'Not now, Kato!' in a high-pitched Clouseau voice, dancing around on one leg, whilst shaking the other, giving him a bucking bronco ride! Considering all the blood we have lost, we still love him and look forward to seeing his cheeky face waiting for us when we get home.

Richard and Ali Watson

Marmalade runt

As a young lad I hankered after a great big ginger tom, the marmalade cat of legend that would rule the roost and defend its master in any sticky situation. Unfortunately, the only ginger kitten we could find was a sickly beast with white paws looking, as I remarked on first viewing, like a well-known cereal standing in a bowl of milk. And so 'Cornflake' entered my life. He only survived his first few months on the planet because my mother refused to let him die, and he was always the weediest cat in the neighbourhood, but I loved him to bits.

Phil Hawks

Rugby tackle

My wife has put a bell on her cat's neck, so that it has an audible means of approach. The cat is called Cooking Fat, and a very apt appellation it is too. She likes nothing better than playing rugby with my wife ('er indoors), tapping her legs from under her when she least expects it, usually in the garden and preferably on a muddy day! When I was a lad we had a cat called Tiddles. My old Aunt Lucy couldn't, or wouldn't, say Tiddles and always had to call it Tibbles, much to my youthful amusement.

Roger Jones

In the spotlight

A friend of mine once had a cat which was black except for the tip of its tail, which was white. He called it Spotlight. I once was adopted by a stray cat which I called Thursday, because that was the day on which he turned up on my doorstep. My current cat is called Orlando, and yes, he's a marmalade.

David Rider

Clumsy cat

A few years ago a colleague of mine acquired a kitten which, as kittens do, kept climbing onto furniture and other things; but this one kept falling off and was consequently christened Tumble.

Peter Collard

Brazilian beverage

During the early '80s after three years in Rio de Janeiro, we promised our children two cats. Being rather fond of Brazilian drinks, we thought of naming them Caipirinha and Caipiroska, but decided this was too long. We therefore decided to give them a shortened version and they became Vodka and Tonic. This was fine until we were calling for them at night, and even worse in the mornings! It also caused raised eyebrows when they were called into the vet's surgery from the waiting room.

Lesley and Peter Diggins

What's in a name?

When I was a year old my mum had a kitten and called it Moses, as it was so miserable. Unfortunately, I couldn't say Moses, so the kitten got called Bowey and the name stuck. Another cat we had was a white called Snowy, but it refused to answer to the name, preferring to answer to Kit-e-Kit.

Anne Baldwin

Speedy cats

We have two wonderful little cats. They are brothers who were
RSPCA rescue cats. Their names are Foggy and Mackenzie,
after the then World Superbike champion, Carl Fogarty and
British Superbike Champion Niall Mackenzie. They are not
particularly catty names, but they would probably give either of
the bikers a good run for their money speed-wise.

Jill Dickinson

Reet petite

In the 1960s my mother's pride and joy was a cat called Teet,
or sometimes, more affectionately, Teets. This was a shortened
form of Petite. He might have been petite when he arrived as a
kitten, but petite he certainly was not when he grew up to be a
huge, plug-ugly bruiser of a tom-cat. Probably to counter the
derision of the other local cats, burdened with such a daft name,
he turned into a mountainous, macho street-fighter, ending up
with two collapsed ears and only one eye!

The worst thing of all, however, was when I was
despatched to get him back into the house. Imagine my chagrin,
as a rather self-conscious teenager at the time, having to stand
out in the street calling out, 'Teet,' or 'Teets'! The neighbours
used to fall about laughing, and the local teenage girls, who
probably thought I was launching a desperate appeal, avoided
me like the plague!

Ken Howard

Bit of a mouthful

My little Burman cross is named Jessica Jezebel Mavis Cruet
Bastable Allen. Jessica was my choice, Jezebel was my son-in-
law's, Mavis Cruet, after the fat little fairy who couldn't fly in the
children's TV programme *Willo the Wisp*; Bastable is my

30

surname and Allen is my daughter's. Jess is now 17 and a half and rules me with a paw of iron in a velvet glove. Her body language is very eloquent; if I upset her, she sits with her back to me, tail curled round all four feet and won't acknowledge me by so much as a flick of the ear!

Margaret Bastable

The perfect gent

We called our cat Mr Micawber, after the Dickens character in *David Copperfield*. He is a stray black and white tom who adopted us three years ago and he still likes us to keep a respectful distance – only I am allowed to stroke his head. He first lived in a makeshift shelter I constructed from boxes and umbrellas, then he moved into the shed; now he is fully resident in the garden porch, for which I have made a three-layer plastic door with a cat flap. The porch is fitted with old carpet, a chair plus folded travel rug, a box and blankets, a litter tray (which he ignores), a heater and his own fire extinguisher! Mr Micawber looks the typical Victorian gentleman, with waxed white whiskers showing up against black chops – altogether a great old character.

Joan Carter

A dream come true?

This is a weird, but true, story that happened when I was about 10 years old. One night, when I was tucked up in bed, I dreamed that a small snake was slithering up to me. I knew I had to grab it before it bit me so, in my dream, I caught hold of it tightly. It bit me anyway, on the hand, before slithering away again. I awoke in a sweat, put on the light and looked at my hand where I'd been 'bitten'. I was gobsmacked to see two neat puncture marks side by side on the back of my hand. Then I saw the culprit. Our cat, very indignant and (sore) tail lashing angrily, was glaring at me from a nearby chair. She'd obviously been sleeping on the bed before I grabbed her tail, and had scratched or bitten me before jumping off.

Jill Wood

Silly cat

My wife and I have had our cat, Jerry, who is a light ginger tom, for 17 years. A few years ago I was preparing spaghetti Bolognese in the kitchen when my wife called me into another room. I left the kitchen for a short while, leaving the ingredients for the meal, all still packed, on the work surface. Upon returning to the kitchen a short while later, I noticed that the minced beef had disappeared. I looked over to the other side of the kitchen, where I could hear a noise coming from under the table. There was our Jerry, with his fangs stuck in the polystyrene tray of mince, unable to remove his teeth and devour the contents. How we laughed!

Matthew Norton

The ship's cats

We got our two cats as ship's cats when we lived on a narrow boat – although they brought on board more beasts than they killed! We named them Hannigan and Redfern, after two brick-layers we had been friendly with before we bought the boat. It came as rather a surprise when, after selling the boat and moving to a farm in Ireland, they both became pregnant. They gave birth on the same night – to eight kittens between them – and we never did know which kitten belonged to whom, as they shared their care throughout.

Caron Garrod

Fish in a flap

One Sunday afternoon I was at my auntie's house when we heard rather a loud commotion coming from the kitchen. When we came to investigate, Smartie the cat (very big) had decided to supplement his diet with a large koi carp. This beautiful ornamental fish, about 12 inches long, was causing Smartie some problems and after five minutes he gave up trying to negotiate it through the cat flap and went to sit smugly in his basket. I'm not sure whether the neighbours ever found out what happened to their fish!

Elizabeth

Carbonated cat

My sister's cat is a Ragdoll called Bollinger, because he bubbles, fizzes (even at five years old) and was jolly expensive! He also gets up my nose, and rules the whole house.

Trisha Woods

Curiosity...

Many moons ago we acquired a cat which, after much deliberation, we called Maharani. My father, who had spent his formative years in India, suggested the name. However, the cat, while possessing many of the graces you'd expect both of a queen and a cat, also possessed a feral streak, meaning that she often didn't return home for a day or two. This unfortunate habit resulted in a number of incidents in which she suffered some form of incarceration.

The first such incident occurred when she was locked in the garage of a newly constructed house by the builders, who kept their tools locked away over the weekend. We had to push food and a shallow saucer of water under the garage door until the builders liberated her. She was there for three days.

The second occurred when she paid a visit to a neighbour who had recently lost her own cat. Maharani went through the cat flap as usual and wandered round the house looking for attention. She went into a bedroom, but the door closed behind her, locking her in. Unfortunately the occupants were away on holiday, and it was three or four days before we discovered where she was and we had to break in to rescue her. Luckily, the neighbours were very understanding.

But the most dramatic of Maharani's incarcerations was when she again disappeared for a few days. I spent several days scouring the site where new houses were being built, to no avail. On returning home following one of these excursions, I heard a muffled mewing. It appeared to be coming from the house next door, which was unoccupied. Fearing another lock-in, I broke a window to gain entry to the house. Calling her name, I could hear the muffled mewing again, but it seemed to be coming from outside this time. However, when I went outside I could hear her inside the house. It soon became clear that she was in the cavity wall! For some time there had been a hole in the wall, through which a drainage pipe was to be fitted. Clearly, Maharani had decided to explore this just around the time it was fitted and the brickwork completed. Some frantic calls to the builder followed by a few bricks being knocked out of the wall finally resulted in a very bedraggled, thin cat emerging from the gloom. A couple of days later, she was back to normal. Despite these incidents, her tendency to wander and explore were never curbed and she retained her 'wild child' streak until the end of her days.

Ashley Jagoe

Extended leave

In November 1958 our family and cat, Sandy, a ginger tom, moved to a new property about five miles away. Sandy's favourite trick was to run up Dad's body and sit across his shoulders – usually when he was not wearing a shirt – much to the hilarity of the rest of the family. We had been settled in the new house for about a year when a real pea-soup fog descended. Much to the dismay of my little sister Wendy, Sandy went missing. He was ten years old and fit, but the weather was awful and at the time there were reports of cat snatching for experiments. After many days of searching we had to accept that Sandy was gone for good.

Another year passed when a pea-souper returned. The family was sitting in the dining room eating the evening meal, when we heard a cat crying at the door. As Dad opened the door, in walked a skinny, dirty ginger tom as though he owned the place. Wendy said it was Sandy, but we all pooh-poohed the suggestion. Nevertheless, Wendy was convinced. In an effort to find out if it was really Sandy, Dad called the cat and tapped his shoulder, and sure enough, the cat ran up his body and sat on his shoulders just as Sandy used to. We needed no further convincing! You can imagine the elation when we realised that this scruffy urchin was really Sandy, skinny and dirty, but basically fit. He lived for another year very happily, spending much time sitting on top of the budgie's cage and letting him pull his fur with his beak.

Terry Dyball

Birds beware

Henry the cat lived with my nieces from the age of eight weeks. At about three or four months Henry was diagnosed by the vet as Henrietta! For various reasons, they could not keep Henri and we adopted her. She is gorgeous, fat and very happy. However, when we first took her to the vet, we realised there was a small problem – she was on their books under her maiden name, which was Henrietta Bird!

Sally J. Attwater

Alley cat

Some years ago a very bedraggled cat entered our lives, and the obvious name to call him was Tramp. With our love and atten-tion, he grew into a very handsome gentleman, his one problem being that he rather liked the ladies. This got him into all sorts of scrapes, and the vet's advice was to have him neutered, which we did as quickly as possible. Some six months later a rather disturbed neighbour came to complain that not only had Tramp broken their cat flap to get at their two female cats who were in season, but his melodic calling had also attracted all the females from miles around, who had all joined in the chorus! Although I assured him that it couldn't possibly be Tramp, he insisted that I should go and look. Sure enough, there stood Tramp, surrounded by some very frisky females. I hastened home to ring the vet. Had he removed his tonsils by mistake? No, the vet assured me – he had removed the rights bits, but as Tramp was an adult cat he still had his memories, but not the wherewithal to do anything about it. The solution was to throw a towel over one very embarrassed cat and bring him home. Strangely enough, the females did produce kittens in due course and one of them was the exact replica of Tramp. Needless to say, Tramp kept very quiet on the subject, but I am happy to report that the memories faded and Tramp lived to the ripe old age of 21.

Joan Sherwood

Thirsty and moody!

Like everyone else having acquired two kittens (both black), we spent several days trying to think up appropriate names. We felt Sooty and Sweep to be a bit too obvious but, as the days went by, we resigned ourselves to them. However, one evening after a glass or two of wine, we were watching one of the kittens who was so small that she seemed to stagger about. So there it was, staring us in the face – Dipsomania! It didn't take long to christen her sister Schizophrenia as she was already showing signs of mood swings – all over us one minute, and the next, giving us a look of utter disdain. They lived up to their names and visits to see the vet always caused much merriment. Skits passed away two years ago, but Dips is now approaching her 19th birthday, and she still staggers a lot!

Alison Sharpe

Clowning around

Shortly after leaving home and moving into her own flat, my daughter Jane visited a pet shop and instantly fell in love with a kitten. She took her home and decided to call her Charlie. A few weeks later, a friend's cat had a litter of kittens and Jane said she would give a home to one of them. She chose a sweet little fellow, and was quite pleased with herself when she thought of the name Chaplin. So Charlie and Chaplin were flatmates, but the day was looming when, if something wasn't done, there would be lots of little Charlie Chaplins running around.

The end of this tale is rather sad, as poor Charlie died after what should have been a straightforward operation. Chaplin has been without his Charlie for several years now, as Jane has never had the heart to replace Charlie.

Christine Carter

Exotic cats

When our lovely ginger cat Boyo died last year we so missed having a cat in the house, that we decided to look for a kitten. We visited all the rescue homes, but none of them had kittens. Our first find was a tiny ginger and white scrap from a local pet shop. He was eight weeks old. In the meantime, my daughter had found an advertisement in the local paper for a kitten for sale. We went off to visit and found a tiny black and white kitten who was only six weeks old. We couldn't resist her, so we brought her home. The next problem was, of course, names. Eventually we settled on Mandu, as in Kathmandu and Eartha, as in Eartha Kitt!

Sheila Gunter

Aptly named

I knew two cats that always caused a certain amount of merriment. One was called Harpic, because he was clean round the bend and the other was called Carpenter, because he did odd jobs around the house!

Katie Lane

Hot cats

Our two cats are called Bhuna and Dhansak – we are never short of a good Indian meal in our house. The alternative was to be Rogue and Josh, but that sounded silly. When the cats go to their 'holiday camp' (or kennels) with Cleo, our Great Dane, they are booked in as Cleo and the Curries, which we think sounds rather like a dodgy '60s group!

Liz Draper

Classical cat

When my daughter Charlotte was in her final year at our local village school, she was thrilled to be able to choose her own kitten from a friend's litter. It was December and as the kitten, a male, was mainly white with a few ginger splodges, we suggested something seasonal such as Noel or Snowflake. However, all our suggestions fell on deaf ears.

At the time Charlotte was busy practising for her grade 5 flute exam. Each day when she practised, the little kitten would clamber up the back of a chair to get close to the source of the music, joining in lustily with loud, appreciative noises. The piece he especially liked was Elgar's 'Chanson du Matin' and so Charlotte decided to call him Elgar, explaining that he had a very musical miaow! Elgar's other passion is sunbathing and, despite all our efforts with sunblock, he had to have his ears removed several years ago. It doesn't seem to have affected him at all, although he does rather resemble a snowy owl when perched on top of the garden wall. His nickname is now Fearless Earless.

Stephanie Poulter

We are not amused

My wife, Donna, and I have three cats at the moment, all of which came from the Cats Protection League. Murphy is a huge ginger and white attention-seeking monster who is frightened of trainers. Before going to the cat shelter to get another one, we had decided that it was set in stone that we didn't want a black cat. We came out with two black moggies, sisters, one with a tiny white bib, and the other with ten white hairs in the same place. It took us a good week or so to name these two. I named Tess first, and then Donna's friend at work jokingly suggested that we call the other one Tickles. We thought it was a smashing idea! We can now shout, 'Tess... Tickles!' out of the back door each night and laugh every time. However, the first day we let them out they went missing. We spent a whole week shouting their names around the local area, and we were definitely not amused.

Chris Phillips

Comedy duo

My two female cats – now four years old – are a proper pair of comedians, so I named them French and Saunders. If they had been boys, they would have been Morecambe and Wise.

Gilly Alexander

Cat scam

We had a very clever cat called Tabby. Not a very imaginative name, but it was the best I could do at the age of four. My mum hates mice and used to reward Tabby with a treat when she caught one. The treat was extra special – cream, chicken or fish – if she caught a mouse in the pantry. Being a smart cat, Tabby quickly realised that catching mice was a good way of getting goodies, and if she caught one in the pantry, the treat was especially nice. She put two and two together. She would stun a mouse in the garden, bring it in and release it in the pantry. The mouse would recover and be trapped in the pantry, to be discovered by Mum the next time she opened the door. Mum would scream and Tabby would rush in (like Tom in the *Tom and Jerry* cartoons), kill the mouse and claim her reward. The scam only failed when I actually saw her doing this and showed Mum what she was up to. I don't think Tabby ever forgave me for ruining her scam.

Phil Barker

Miracle cat

Our son Owen brought a feral kitten home. It was only about two weeks old, its eyes all gummed up and in a terrible state, and the vet said it would almost certainly die. Owen fed her every two to three hours with a doll's feeding bottle, and miraculously she survived. She is called Miep for two reasons. The first is that it was the name of Anne Frank's sister, and Owen was reading *The Diary of Anne Frank* at the time; and the second is that she couldn't

miaow – 'meep' is the only noise she could make. She had a l
and we kept a tom kitten. He is absolutely massive now and named
Weasel, after *Catweazel* from the children's programme.

Robert and Julia Turner

Aristocat

We had lost our previous cat less than a month, when a friend
of ours who worked for the Royal parks rang us to say that one
of his staff had found a bewildered puss in the flowerbeds on the
roundabout in Parliament Square. He asked if I would like him,
but I said no, as it was too soon after losing Smokey. Faced with
the possibility of him being put down if he went to the RSPCA
and wasn't claimed, I relented and he arrived with us that
evening. We called him Churchill, as he was found next to the
statue of Sir Winston Churchill.

At first, Churchill was very timid and hid under a cupboard for
two days, only coming out when the men of the family
persuaded him. It was obvious he didn't like women, but I soon
changed that. We took him to the vet, who said he was in a very
poor state and the kindest thing would be to have him put down.
We did not, and Churchill spent five happy years as a member
of the family, winning the hearts of all he met. Churchill was a
very aristocratic cat, sitting up at the table with us at meal times
and much preferring our food to his tinned variety.
Coincidentally, he was ginger and we live near Chartwell where
Churchill lived and where he always kept ginger cats.

Annie Williams

Dictator cats!

My colleague told me that, in the 1950s, her Latin teacher had
named her two cats Kitler and Pussolini!

Sandra Murray

Name change

About a year ago we acquired two cats from a shelter and decided to call them Nelson and Winnie. The female was made to feel unwelcome by her brother and subsequently left. Soon afterwards, Nelson was found hanging by one of his back legs in a hedge, still alive, presumably having had an accident after a bird-chasing spree. I phoned my wife, who worked in a cashmere shop in St Andrews, to convey the sad news and asked her to bring a box home to take him to the vet.

We duly took him to the vet and left him there for the night. The next day we phoned to enquire about his condition, and were informed that 'Shorts' had had a comfortable night. Not wanting to appear stupid, we asked her to repeat what she'd said. After all, who was Shorts? She repeated her remark and went on to explain that that was the name on the box. My wife had emptied out a load of tartan shorts from a box, so we could use it to take him to the vet! So we now have only one cat, and his name is Shorts.

Iain M. G. Reid

Travelling cat

Gulliver wasn't much to look at – just a black cat with his tail forever pointing towards heaven, but what he lacked in looks, he made up for in character. He was given to us at eight weeks old, and when he arrived he explored every nook and cranny of his new home, and my young son named him, very aptly, Gulliver. He came shopping with me, tail in the air, went to school with my son, went to church with my daughter and accompanied me to my evening job as a hotel receptionist. He used to sleep in the filing tray until it was time to go home.

One weekend we went away and left him in the care of a neighbour. On our return, our neighbour was frantic as Gulliver had been missing for the whole weekend, but suddenly he turned up on our return. It wasn't until I went to work the next evening that I was told he had moved in to the hotel for the weekend, where he was known and loved by the staff. In fact, when we moved they begged us to let them have him, but we didn't! Gulliver came with us and soon made himself known to the new neighbours, and knew that by begging on his hind legs, like a dog, he would get plenty of titbits.

Ruby Mayers

Absent cat

Some friends of my daughter's with two children increased their family by adding a kitten. They couldn't agree on a name until the kitten learnt to hide from the children, when it became Egon – because the children kept saying, 'Where's 'e gone?'

Roy Turner

Punctual cat

My greatly loved cat was called D.C. (that darn cat)! D.C. could tell the time, always appearing at 10 p.m. for cornflakes and then to bed.

Joan Roberts

Smelly cat!

Our eldest son, then a teenager, bought himself a 'pet shop' kitten, which suffered from a 'smelly bottom' when young. She was promptly named Poo Face. Some time later, my wife and I were on the Greek island of Kos and when we phoned home, the boys told us that she had given birth on the younger son's bed and they had decided which kitten to keep – its name was to be Frogg. Our other cat is now rather elderly, but his name was chosen by the best method I know. The four of us wrote down all the names we could think of and put them in an ice bucket (having first drunk the wine). Each name was taken out in turn and read out – if we all disliked it, it was destroyed. We were then left with a short list of names from which we selected Gizmo, shortened to Gizzy.

Tony Kent-Francis

Shed cats

When we moved into our house 22 years ago, there were two black kittens under the shed. We named them Mum and Dad and, after a few years, Mum got as far as venturing into the kitchen. After she had her first litter, she kept them very well hidden until one day, when she took us to see them. We kept one, calling it Death-Wish, due to the fact that it enjoyed perching on fences and annoying not only ours, but all the neighbours' dogs, who used to spend ages jumping up to try and get him down, whilst he sat there with a supercilious look on his face. When he got bored with this, he used to climb the side of the house and cry piteously so that people going past would knock to ask why we didn't get him down.

When the next set of kittens came along, the one we kept was called Two-Stroke, because of the very high level of noisy purring. He could easily drown out the best TV or radio programme, and was even worse when he draped himself around either of our necks. Sadly, none of them are with us any more, but we have very fond memories.

Rosemarie Ford

Get it right!

A friend of mine told me a wonderful story. Her husband is from Sligo, in the west of Ireland, and in that town there is a family called the Gillens. One of the boys took the dog, Skippy, to see the vet. When it came round to their turn, the vet came out and said: 'Skippy Gillen?' The lad stood up and said: 'No, this is Skippy O'Donovan, it's my mother-in-law's dog'!

Barbara Basham

Famous four

I have a pride of four cats. The head cat is called Pyewacket – the name came from the play *Bell, Book and Candle*. Pyewacket's mother was a Burmese and his father was a pure-bred moggie from Scotland, and he is dark chocolate brown. He is now 11 and his age and wisdom make him the perfect head cat. The next one in seniority is called Merlin, who got his name because he can disappear in mid-miaow, unlock cat flaps, open certain types of window latches and escape from just about anywhere. His alias is The Hairy Houdini. He is very good at the unsolicited purr, that is, the purr that starts even though nobody is touching him or even in the same room!

Next comes Esmeralda, who is named after Granny Weather-wax in the Terry Pratchett *Discworld* novels. Esme got the name because she is very prim and proper just like Granny. Finally, there is the bimbo. She is an absolute disgrace to the cat world; the lights are on, but nobody is home. I named her Magnificat because of her long hair and sea-green eyes. Nifi is a chinchilla cross, but the brains got lost somewhere.

Debra Keasal

Proper charmers

My little monsters are called Charlie and Angel. They were already named when I got them from the Park House Animal Sanctuary near Canterbury. It's not, as you'd imagine, a reference to the TV series. Angel was one of the many unfortunate statistics, handed in to the sanctuary pregnant and unwanted. Her name is a reflection on both her beautiful, pure white coat and her sweet nature. Whilst at the sanctuary, she gave birth to three kittens. Two found homes easily, but the third, a proper Charlie, had put off potential companions with his habit of chewing fingers. None the worse for their long stay, the two set about a somewhat aggressive campaign of affection (and chewing of fingers) and I couldn't have left without them. Mother and son continue to charm everyone they meet.

Wayne Spillett

New name

Our cat was abandoned twice before we gave him a home. He had been named Scratty by the cats' home, but I decided that I was not going to stand at the door at night shouting 'Scratty', so we had to think of something else. During his first two weeks with us, he completely lost his old fur, the hair coming off in handfuls as I groomed him. Hence, the name Samson. He is now a lovely affectionate cat, and very telepathic.

Carol from Harrogate

Tough cats?

When my partner Tim (now my husband) and I first moved in together, we decided it was time to start a family. I contacted the local RSPCA to see if we could adopt two kittens. After lots of discussion about types and breeds, we decided on two black kittens. Our RSPCA lady was extremely helpful and managed to find us a litter within a matter of days, but the kittens wouldn't be ready for about three weeks. This gave us bags of time to think about names. Not wanting to have a couple of softies, we had in mind that our two cats would be 'bruisers', ruling the neighbourhood, and no one would beat them up. So we spent many hours thinking of famous male twosomes. Finally, we arrived at Ronnie and Reggie (the Kray twins). Welcome to the toughest cats on the block!

When we went to collect the kittens, we found in the basket two of the tiniest, most pathetic bundles of fluff you have ever seen. It was love at first sight for all four of us. Needless to say, the hard man names didn't stick – from then on they were known as Stanley and Oliver (Laurel and Hardy)!

Julie Wilkinson

Not tonight...

Ten years ago I opened the back gate and a little face appeared. It was tiny, black, very thin and covered in fleas. My husband gave it lots of milk and the tuna that I had put in our sandwiches. The cat was then put outside. It was still there in the morning and in the following days it made a bed in the flower box outside the back door. Eventually we made it a proper bed to sleep in and it became a much-loved member of the family.

After finding out it was a female, our son, then 16, suggested that it should be called Josephine, as in 'Not tonight, Josephine', when the kitten wanted to stay in our home the first night she appeared.

Anonymous

Confused cats

Over the years, two of my cats have had rather silly names. My black one was called Snowy, and the white one was called Sooty!

Roz Stacey

Sporty cats

Being a very sporting household with golf being the predominant activity, our two cats are named with this sporting connotation in mind. Peter is a very large, long-haired black and white moggie with huge whiskers, extra large feet and all four white spatted. Alice is small, very pretty, almost a British Blue, but also a moggie. Thus, when being called in for their meals, the call goes out: 'Peter, Alice, dinner!' Both of them spend many happy hours curled up in the conservatory, which is warm and sunny in the winter, and extremely hot in the summer. Some time ago, a somewhat battered ginger tom visited and became quite friendly with Peter and Alice, to the extent that he would curl up with them in the conservatory, share whatever food was on offer and became part of the household cat population. We did think he was a stray, but it turned out he was an inveterate scrounger. Thus we had Peter, Alice and Ernie! Any golf fan will appreciate this.

Pip Vyvyan

Cleaning cat

I was allowed to have my first cat at the age of eight and was allowed to choose his name, but what should it be? On arriving at his new home, the very first thing he did was to climb into and proceed to demolish my mother's magnificent arrangement of fresh, plump bulrushes. The name problem was solved – it had to be Moses!

We now have a gorgeous apricot and white fluffy moggie, who was found along with his mother, cold, soaking wet and starving in a humane trap, which had not been checked. He was, of course, quite wild and terrified of everyone and everything. We called him Harford Bridge, after the area of Norwich from where he was rescued. However, our daughter had other ideas. Because he polished off every morsel of food given to him, his dishes were always sparkling clean and not a single dropped crumb escaped his attention. Our floors were always immaculate and so Helen referred to him as the family's new hoover and Hoover is what he has answered to ever since.

Ann Youngman

Liberated kitten

Back in 1966 our neighbour was a bookkeeper for our local vet. One day she came home with a sad story of a kitten that had been left to be spayed and had not been collected by her owners. Sadder still, it became apparent that the owners had left a fictitious name and address, the name being Robinson. Week after week we were advised that 'Pussy Cat Robinson' was still there and, despite the offer 'free to a good home', no one had come forward. One day our neighbour came round to us more distraught than usual, as the vet had said that if no one wanted her by the end of the week, they would have no option but to put her to sleep. Our neighbour was unable to have her because of her dogs, so my husband and I succumbed.

The next day we were the proud owners of a six-month-old black and white kitten. We felt that Pussy Cat Robinson was a bit of a mouthful, so we decided to rename her. Our daughter, then aged seven, said that we should call her Freda. 'Why Freda?' we enquired. 'Because we "freed her" from being put to sleep.' This stuck and we enjoyed a very happy 13 years with our Freda.

Rita Fogg

A what?

I lived in Hong Kong for many years and had an assortment of cats there at various times, but one was particularly special. I was walking home from work one day, when a tiny bit of ginger fluff jumped from under a parked car and landed on my foot. I placed it back under the car and walked on for 50 yards. Then I turned round, walked back, picked up the smallest kitten I'd ever seen and took her home. I had a lovely Chinese boyfriend at the time, and we stood and looked at this minute and very dirty bit of a kitten sitting on the palm of my hand. 'She is so tiny,' I said. 'What shall we call her?' My boyfriend amazed me with his knowledge of English vocabulary (my Cantonese being very limited!) when he said, instantly: 'Amoeba.' I loved the name immediately. It was often shortened to Meebs, Meeba and Meebles, but she was always officially Amoeba.

Jean Grundy

Bath cat

My daughter Hillary, along with her fellow students at Huddersfield University, used to feed a cat whom they called Manky Bath Mat – because that's what he resembled.

Pat from Plymouth

Rough beginnings

Years ago, I used to work in the office at a local factory and I found a lovely little grey cat straying in the factory grounds. She was being fed scraps by the factory workers. I felt so sorry for her that one lunchtime, I picked her up, popped her into my jacket, and took her home. As she was a dark grey, like the colour of emery paper, with all the sparkles and glints that go with it, I called her Emery, soon to be shortened to Emmy. As a Russian Blue, she was rather silent, not often given to miaowing. Instead, she had subtle ways of making herself 'heard', such as little pats with her paw, or a meaningful stare with her bright green eyes. I had her for 16 years, by which time she must have been at least 18 and she is still missed now.

Karen René

Love is the drug!

My two cats, Prozac and Valium, are my friends and family and the best drugs that anyone could have – very addictive, but harmless!

Sheila Gurner

Big boy

The cat next door is called Uggle Barmsby! He is a big, black tom-cat and he weighs more than a stone.

Mrs E. Jones

Cul-de-cat

I live in a lovely cul-de-sac with some really super neighbours and am surrounded by cats. Mine is Rosie; Mitzi lives across the road; next door, the vicar has two cats, Moses, and Zippi (after Zipporah, Moses' wife). Next to them live Archibald and Arthur and opposite them are Wookie and Pebbles. Backing on to our garden is our local vet with her cats, Annie, who has only one eye, and Denis, the local ginger thug!

Patricia Banks

Psychic friends

My first cat, a black mini-panther, all teeth and claws, was called Tommy Bodkin, though after an operation on a hind leg, he had to wear a plastic 'flowerpot' round his neck to stop him pulling stitches out. He was then nicknamed 'Bucket Head' and 'Thomas a Bucket'.

Cat number two was a poorly, but gorgeous, little grey and white cat. He was wheezy, blind in one eye and had had a broken leg at some point, because it hadn't set properly and the leg was stiff. While living with me, he fell out of a tree and fractured his pelvis and eventually he also lost the sight of his good eye. What other name could he have had but Scruffy Cat?

The third and current cat is white with a black tail. He is the most laid-back creature I have ever met, extremely affectionate and cuddly, and always purring contentedly. Though he is really a short-haired cat, his coat is long and very fine. When you stroke him, the hairs come out in handfuls and float around in the air. His name is Fergus Percival – Fergus for the fur, and Percival for the purr! He is so laid-back he will be a hard act to follow. However, my furry feline friends seem to know when there is a cat needed in the house, as Scruffy and Fergus walked in at exactly the right time, which is why I call them my psychic friends.

Evelyn Inglis

Mixed-up cat

Our cat is called Angus Farqharson MacGregor. Angus, because he is jet black and we hail originally from Aberdeen; Farqharson because he is a real poser; and MacGregor because he is a thug (know your Scottish history?).

Edith

Married cat bliss

We have had seven cats over our married life, three of whom arrived complete with names, and four we have named ourselves. Dizzy was a female, inherited from my sister, named after Dizzy Gillespie. Simon was named after Simon Williams, the actor, when he was in *Colditz* on TV. We then got three kittens and, inspired by DJ Adrian Love, who talked about his 'cat Amaran', decide to name them Cat-Astrophe (Astra for short), Kat-Treena (Treena for short) and Oedie-Puss (shortened to Oedie or sometimes, Edith).

We then decided to adopt from the RSPCA so now have two females: Alice, aged 11, who is noble, long-legged and takes everything in her stride; and Myrtle, aged six, a pretty, chubby tabby who's a bit skittish. Apparently they used to live with Doris and Moriarty!

Helen and Roger Nicholls

Where there's muck...

Many years ago when on an annual visit to Arisaig on the west coast of Scotland for camping/caravan holidays, we made a trip to Eigg and Muck. When we arrived at the latter, we took a walk across the island and, on our return were accosted by a couple of young girls selling white kittens. One of the other passengers bought one and immediately called it Lord Muck. We bought one too, and had to consider alternatives and eventually came up with Mr McMewick. We took him back to Scotland for at least a couple of years after that, to the same camp, and he thoroughly enjoyed searching for mice, or just lazing in the sun with us.

Colin Burchett

Cat doing time

I work as a senior prison officer in Suffolk and the prison cat (now deceased) was called Porridge. Not very original, but he did a good job of guarding the establishment, keeping those that should be in, in and those that should not be in, out ... the mice and rats, that is.

Karl Gibbs

Scaredy cat

My cat's name is Boo, so named because as a kitten he was afraid of his own shadow. Now he is older, he is a little more adventurous.

Angela Davies

Trick name

As a child, I had a Manx cat with the ridiculous name of Guess. When anyone asked his name, we replied, 'Guess,' so they did; there were suggestions of Tiger, Stripey etc. 'No,' would be the reply, 'Guess', and so it went on.

Simon and Linda Levitt

Not a nice cat

16 years ago we acquired a black feral kitten. She was quite evil, even at such a young age, so we called her Fagin, after the character in *Oliver Twist*. When we told the vet her name, she said, 'That's not a very nice name.' 'No,' I replied, 'but then, she's not a very nice cat!' Coincidentally, a year after her adoption of us, we moved to Oliver's Close!

John Howat

Rainy arrival

Our cat goes by the name of Miggy, but his official name is Miguel Indurain. This is because he was given to us by our daughter on the day the Spanish cyclist of that name won the Tour de France for the fifth time. It was a very wet and windy day, and we usually tell people he arrived 'in-de-rain'! He is also referred to as His Imperial Preciousness, as the house seems to revolve around him.

Pat and Roger Moore

Humorous cats

Our first cat was born in the lawnmower grass box in our porch, and was conventionally named Boots, being a tabby with four white feet. But then we heard of someone who called their black cat Snowball, on the basis that there would not be many black cats answering to such a name. This sounded like a good idea and also appealed to our warped sense of humour.

We started in a small way. Our next cat was black and called Tigger. Then we had a ginger cat with four white feet called Takkies – Afrikaans for trainers. After that, we got a tabby called Squiggle, because when we got him as a kitten he was a bit unsteady on his back legs and his bum used to squiggle about.

Our current cat is called Bacon. No literary reference here – he is black and white with a streak down his nose —but the rest of the family objected to Streaky, so Bacon he became.

Chris Holman

Deaf cat

Our cat is mainly white with black splodges, named Deecy. Her full name is AC/DC and she is deaf as a post.

Margaret Handy

Don't ask

My cats are named Philip Schofield and Six. It's best if you don't ask why.

Louise Williams

'Arf a mo!

We currently have Buster – fat, black and white – named after Buster Keaton; and Freddie (originally Freda, but renamed after a visit to the vet!). Previously we had Troxy, named after a long-gone East End cinema and Jasper (ginger, named after Jasper Carrott).

A dear departed friend of mine called Pam had cats called Arthur and Mo, so she could stand in the garden calling 'Arf a mo'. These cats were actually born in Pam's living room whilst we were playing bridge one evening.

My grandparents had a cat just after the war called Sergeant. My husband's parents had a cat that loved a fight and was therefore named Rocky, after Rocky Marciano. My granddaughter, when asked at the age of five what she wanted to call a lovely grey kitten, decided on Nigel! Heaven knows what goes through the minds of children.

Ruth Harris

Trekkie cat

We inherited a cat from my son when he went to Australia called Spock, which still embarrasses me whenever we go to the vet's!

Sandra Tiernan

Barrel, comedian, poet...

One of our cats, a 15-year-old black and white moggie, is called Firkin, because when she was little she looked just like a small barrel. Milligan is a chocolate tabby point Siamese and had very spiky fur, so 'Spike' turned into 'Milligan'. Eliot, a seal point Siamese, is a very literary chap and was named after T.S. Eliot.

Jay Dunford

Winking cat

Many years ago when I was a young girl, we had a kitten who would wink at me, so I called her Winkie. Later on, we were given a farm cat on Mop night (the night of an annual street fair in Warwickshire), so she became Moppet. Her daughter, a tiny jet-black kitten, had the hugest green eyes I had ever seen, so I called her Jade.

Heidi Edgington

Snake or cat?

The most memorable of our cats was called Python. We already had a budgie called Monty. Our neighbour was horrified when she learned what we were going to call the cat and suggested Blackie, as she was jet-black. However, we would not be persuaded and Python lived to the ripe old age of 19. We thought nothing of her unusual name until the day I had to collect her from the vet's. Sitting in the waiting room, to my horror I became an object of amusement when the receptionist called out 'Python Furneaux!'

Peter Furneaux

Cat hotel

My feline friends include my tabby and white, aged eight, who is called Leo. I've had him since he was 12 weeks old and he was the start of my love affair with the feline fraternity.

Pawsha is a big, black female with attitude and will only come to you when she wants to. She likes to have breakfast between 4 and 5 a.m. and if she doesn't get noticed, she will chase poor Leo around.

Panther moved in about four years ago. He would nearly always sleep outside and liked to get in the car when I was parking. On one occasion I had been to the supermarket and had put the shopping in the footwell on the passenger side. I had just pulled up outside the house, opened the driver's door and reached over for the shopping. When I sat back I felt a tap on my shoulder. I slowly turned around, not knowing what to expect, and there was Panther sitting on the back seat! I never did find out where he came from.

The latest arrival is Tramps, who is quite tatty and turns up occasionally to eat the food that Leo and Pawsha have left. He has been known to sleep over as well, and could probably do with a trip to the vet, but I can't get close enough to him yet. My sister reckons the local cats have a hotline advertising my house as the place where you'll get fed and looked after!

Isabel Sweet

Leonine cat

Our cat, a very handsome British Blue, is called Aslan after the lion in the children's book by C.S. Lewis, *The Lion, The Witch and The Wardrobe*.

Michael and Margaret Boyles

Ooh, Betty!

My beautiful tabby cat was called Betty – funny on its own, but even funnier when matched with my surname – Burrell! That usually caused a few sniggers in the vet's waiting room.

Joanne Burrell

Well matched

We have a cat called Pickle and were recently adopted by a stray, whom my daughter has named Branston!

Rosemarie Jarman

Important cats

I was given a black and white kitten as a successor to Katherine O'Cat, who reached the age of 21. I was told it was a queen and took her to the vet for her jabs. When I asked when I should bring her in to be spayed, the vet said that would be difficult, as it was a tom! We had been calling her Katy Too, so this had to be changed to Lord Kitchener – what else would you call a cat with excessively long whiskers that lives in the kitchen? When we got another kitten we called him General Smuts. He went missing one March and reappeared the following November sporting a broken shoulder. Many vet's bills later, he still has a limp but manages to patrol the garden quite well.

Lynda Lynch

Sweet cats

When the children were small we adopted a ginger kitten from the CPL. On leaving, the very kind lady in charge said: 'You won't call him Ginger, will you?' 'Oh, no,' I replied, 'he's got a name to go with my surname.' I was Betty Beale in those days and we called the kitten Bumble, as we thought Bumble Beale was rather sweet. Since then I've been widowed and remarried and I now have two new cats to go with my new name. They are Min and Toes and my surname is now Nuttall!

Betty Nuttall

Tasty cat

My cat is called Honey Yum-Yum. He is gorgeous and I love him to bits!

Joan M. Grigg

Cat-strut

Some years ago, when I was living in Luton, I adopted a big,
black tom-cat, although 'abducted' would probably be more accu-
rate. He lived in the house opposite, but often crossed the road
and strayed into my garden. One day, I noticed a huge lump on
his head, almost like an egg. I knew he'd have to go to the vet's
and I also knew that his owners wouldn't bother to take him. I
rang my own vet and asked her to bring a cage, adding that he
was very big and had talons instead of claws. So off he went to
the vet's to have his abscess drained, which took almost a week,
after which the vet brought him back, and he immediately confis-
cated an armchair as his own. He sat 18 inches high, almost like
a huge black statue and was wonderfully in proportion. Owing to
his habit of walking with what I called a 'gunfighter's swagger', I
named him Jesse James! You could almost hear his spurs jingling.

Karen René

Desperate cat

Three years ago, homeless and injured, in a thunderstorm, he
cried loudly at my kitchen door. I called him Dan because he was
desperate.

Marjory Myers

Clever cats

I own four cats. Caspar and Merlin are black and white twins,
who think they rule the house. But the real boss is Kitty Scarlett,
a very flirtatious tabby, and mother of Tanya Tucker – we were
going through our country and western phase when she was
born! All four are highly intelligent and have completely
taken over.

Anne McLaughlin

Inseparable sisters

When my old cat Daffodil died (so named because she was large and beautiful), I asked the CPL for new 'house cats'. I live on a busy road and have lost several cats to traffic in the past, which is heartbreaking, and they said I'd have to wait, as there aren't many in our area (rural Staffordshire). Three months later they called and all at once had four house cats who needed homes. They had a pair of delightful sisters, whom they would not split, so I took them both. Their names were Pongo and Purdey, but they are now Thelma and Louise and still inseparable.

Helen Rowett

Him or her?

We had a beautiful tom kitten and called him Harvey, after a neighbour's brother. The compulsory visit to the vet to remove his bounce led to 'him' being renamed Harvey Maria. Harvey Maria was followed by two more tom kittens, George and Sidney, though George had kittens and was promptly renamed Georgina. We were never very good at sexing cats, but were thankfully more successful with our children!

Peter Eccles

Strange pairs

Over the years, I've had a few cats, but always in pairs. Their names reflect my interest in cooking and gardening, hence: Catkin and Pussy-Willow; Parsley and Basil; Gary-Baldi and Gingernut (rather thick, so mostly called Nutty); Squeaky-Weaky (she could not miaow) and Five (named after the table number she was found under as a kitten)!

Ali D

One-eyed cat

I am now 81, but in the 1920s we had a cat with only one eye. My parents decided to call him Polyphemus, after the mythical one-eyed giant!

Margaret Hall

Dusty cat

My cat Thomas is an all-white short-haired female. The reason for this is that when she was acquired, she was thought to be a boy, but in time 'grew' and, needless to say, reproduced. Consequently, her name stuck, so we're always explaining. Her daughter is called Abbey, after someone in a TV programme. Next is Tynan, named after Tommy Tynan, the football player, and last is Cobweb. When he was a kitten he was forever getting behind the freezer and cupboards, only to emerge covered in cobwebs!

Sylvia Paskins

Heavenly cat

Several years ago a friend told me that she was looking after the cat belonging to the local Roman Catholic priest while he was away on holiday. This cat rejoiced in the name Magnificat!

Valerie Upson

Noisy cat

A few years ago my daughter Jane was adopted by a handsome brown Burmese cat. He started by visiting, decided he liked the accommodation, so took up residence. He was extremely and loudly vocal, so we christened him Gungha, because he made such a din!

Joyce Moseley

This old man...

We recently acquired a 10-week-old rescue kitten and it took us three weeks to find a suitable name for her. After much deliberation, we decided to call her after our late Old English Sheepdog, Flossie, as she reminded us of her so much. The name in itself may not be quirky but, going back a few years, the mother dog was named Paddy Wak. She had pups, one of whom we kept, and one of the children named it Knick Knack. You can imagine the comments as we would call the dogs while out, 'Knick Knack, Paddy Wak,' and some bright spark would usually reply, 'Give the dog a bone!'

Brian and Jane

King cat

11 years ago I became the proud owner of two silver tabby kittens whom I called Sonny and Cher. A few years later, I acquired a beautiful tortoiseshell kitten whom I named Cilla. Unfortunately, Cilla was killed by a car when she was just over a

year old, but shortly afterwards a close friend brought me another kitten. This one was a tiny spitting ball of completely white fluff. Unnamed, and brought up on a farm without any of the niceties of normal domestic cats, he was a real character, but I also needed to name him in keeping with his older housemates. I called him Elvis! He is now four, and comes for walks with me when I take the dog and brings many 'friends' to play. His biggest mistake was a live pigeon, which he somehow managed to drag through the cat flap and up the stairs into my daughter's bedroom, where it sat, bleeding copiously and cooing angrily at Elvis, who finally realised he had bitten off more than he could chew. He is very well known in our neighbourhood, and basks in the adoration of local children and other cat lovers.

Sally Whittingham

Squirrel cat

When I get a kitten, I like to live with them for a while before naming them, as their characters usually end up suggesting a name. The first kitten had a habit of acting like a squirrel and sitting up on her back legs and smelling the air with her nose twitching – she became Twitch. The next cat was called Cheeky, for obvious reasons. The latest kitten looks just like she has been coloured using a jar of piccalilli, so she is now Pickle.

Peter Gillespie

The longest name?

A while ago we had a pure white cat and he was named after my favourite chocolate at the time, Toblerone. However, we modified the name a little and he became Toby-la-Rone – Toby for short. He was quite a character too. When we moved, we were advised to keep him in for a few days. However, when we let him out he went missing. We thought we had lost him for good, but he turned up three months later at our old house 10 miles away, none the worse for his adventure. The next cat we had caused quite a lot of argument in the naming department between my three children and my friend's two. I used to look after my friend's children after school and when the kitten arrived, so did the arguments about what he would be called.

Eventually, we managed to agree on Benson Alexander Gizmo Edwards!

Sandra Edwards

Up the Blues!

My sister Heather has a beautiful British Blue cat. His name is Stamford, after Stamford Bridge, the football ground of Chelsea F.C. She named him this because her late husband Mick supported Chelsea and the team strip is blue.

Christine Barnes

Sweet names

When my first kitten arrived 25 years ago I had no idea what to call him. Friends kept phoning to ask after him. I had to describe him to them and took to saying that he was 'mainly white, with a round tabby mark on his back. No, not a spot, more like a Polo mint.' So Polo he became for all his 16 years. In the meantime, my father died and I inherited an incontinent Jack Russell called Candy. Candy was still with me when my next two kittens arrived. As I run the village post office, newsagent and sweet shop, I wanted to keep the sweet theme for their names. I rather liked Callard and Bowser, but Sam my husband thought that Bowser was too dog-like. Rowntree and Macintosh was my next choice, but Sam was keen on Snicker and Mars. Nothing was decided and we got a new bed and lovely soft blanket for the kittens' arrival. However, they had other ideas. I had a large, empty terracotta trough on the floor in the sitting room waiting to be potted up. This, they decided, was kitty heaven, and took up residence. The only thing we could call two kittens living in a flowerpot was Bill and Ben! They have, of course, moved on to sleeping on our bed. I use the term 'our bed' in its loosest sense, as we are allowed to sleep in it, provided we arrange ourselves around them.

Rhonda Surman

Cat from Dallas

At 7.30 every evening our black cat, Max, would suddenly take off and fly around the room from table to chair to bookcase, hence his name, the Blue Max. Max had a chum, a big black and white tom who had an American family and lived next door. These two cats would each tap on the window for the other to come out and play and Max's feline friend was called J.R. Mewing!

Margaret Smith

Lost tail

When I was little I was given a black kitten and I called her Madame Tussaud, but she turned out to be a boy, so he became Adam Tussaud. This was really quite apt because, thanks to an unfriendly dog, he lost most of his tail, so I explained to everyone that he had no 'M' at the beginning of his name because he had no tail!

Bobbin Eaglen

Clucking cat!

We named the little tortoiseshell kitten who bounded happily into our garden, Chicken, as the sound she made was more like a cluck than a miaow! Little did we know that she had decided to make her home with us, or perhaps we would have given the name more thought. We did feel very foolish whenever we were asked her name at the vet's, and latterly told them it was Dicken to save our blushes!

Patricia Aspinall

Can I come in?

One of my cats, sadly no longer with us, was called Leo. He was a large ginger tom with long hair and fully stretched out he would cover half the length of our three-seater sofa. During the summer months he liked to sit with me on the doorstep holding an ice cream cornet in his paws, normally vanilla. His main trick, however, when he wanted to come in and there was no window open, was to knock on the front door! He would do this by jumping up and holding on with his paws and then he would push away with his back legs, thus knocking on the door! Our milkman couldn't believe it when he witnessed this for himself.

Paul G

A-tissue!

Our own cat, a lovely cream ginger moggie, is called Two-Ply. She was bought for our daughter Claire by a friend 11 years ago. She came from a pet shop and we were assured that she had had her injections, but soon afterwards she started to sneeze continually. Claire said she needed a box of tissues and eventually decided that Two-Ply was a very apt name for her.

Betty Smith

Manx stray

Cats came into my life when I was just two years old and we had moved to an old house where an elderly lady had lived. Her dear puss Bobtail adopted us when we moved in. He would come and share our fish paste sandwiches, which we ate in the garden while my Dad and Uncle were doing up the house. He was a real Manx cat with a tiny tail and a wonderful affectionate nature. He would let Mum lay her sewing all over him when he sat on her knee and would come and lie at the foot of our beds if we were poorly. Each morning he climbed up the old pear tree outside Mum and Dad's bedroom to ask to be let in. He had two little stray friends who came to see us from time to time – we named them Halfy and Three Quarters, because of the lengths of their tails!

Mary from Stratford

Easter bunny!

We have a very large, fat cat who is all white, named Bunny because he arrived on Easter Sunday.

Lynda Lomas

The last straw!

Our cat is a thief, but no ordinary thief. No roast beef, bacon or chicken for Reggie. Ronnie, his brother, looks at him in disgust. Ronnie is a posh cat, and a shining example of what all pedigree cats should be like. Lithe, sleek, quick and very aristocratic, he stalks and kills his prey with perfect skill and timing, while sneering at Reggie. Reggie, on the other hand, doesn't know he is a pedigree cat. If he were to read, the *Beano* would be his level. His level of fitness is akin to a couch potato. He sleeps most of the day, and seems to think, 'Why hunt, when you can have it brought to you in a bowl?' He did once catch something, since when his prize has become his passion. The only slight problem is that Reggie doesn't seem to know that his prize is an inanimate object. He has now discovered exactly where they live and steals them at any opportunity. His passion is ... drinking straws. If either of my daughters has a can of Coke or other drink and leaves it unattended for a brief period, Reggie will steal away the straw. The straws are kept in the cereal cupboard and if it is left open, even momentarily, he'll be in there rooting about like a pig hunting for truffles! But where do the straws go? He hides them under one of the two rugs in our dining room. Once I was shocked to find 18 straws under one of the rugs, but to this day I don't know why he loves them so much.

Louise Starks

Flying cat

Earlier this year my son's girlfriend stayed the night, as they were going on holiday the next day. After they had left for the airport early on Sunday morning, I was working upstairs on my computer when I suddenly realised I had not seen our blue point Ragdoll cat, called Linford, for some time. I called him, but there was no response, so I shouted down to my wife to see if she had seen him. She hadn't. I got up to investigate and, walking on to the landing I saw the bedroom door open where my son's girlfriend had slept. I thought he must be under the bed, so I pushed open the door to have a look and, to my horror, the bedroom window was open. I rushed to the window, looked down the 18 feet to the lawn and there he was, sitting on the grass. He had either jumped or fallen. I ran downstairs, asking my wife on the way if she had seen Linford flying past the window. I picked him up and a visit to the vet confirmed there was no damage done, but I came away £25 lighter!

Michael Exley

Leap of faith

Henry Gresham CBE came to stay with us when his owner was posted abroad. The latter was an OBE, so Henry became a Cat of the British Empire. He was large, formally dressed in black and white, friendly in a dignified way and took to arriving in the living room with one bound onto the coffee table which had a glass insert in the top, from which he would survey his new family with kindly approbation. The glass made him slide a bit, but he braked with straight legs like an aircraft landing on a carrier. It was a virtuoso performance, understated, yet supremely elegant.

One day our small daughter managed to crack the glass insert and for reasons of safety we removed it. When Henry appeared he made his usual gigantic leap into the air, sailed across the room, put his feet down for the deck landing and hit fresh air. With a total loss of dignity, he flopped into the space in the centre of the table and onto a lower wooden shelf, his whiskers against the upper level and his eyes wide open in amazement. He was overcome with embarrassment, hopped out rapidly and stalked away bushy tailed. He stopped at the door, sat down, licked a back leg while glancing over his left shoulder to see if we had noticed. He marched out and only then did we dare to laugh!

Alan and Jeanne

Tess the tom

Finding myself unable to have a dog, I was persuaded to have one of my friend's kittens. I selected a beautiful blue-grey she-kitten and we became good friends very quickly. I named her Tess (of the D'Urbervilles). When she reached the appropriate age, I booked her in to the vet's for injections, where Tess was pronounced to be a very healthy tom! Our relationship shifted slightly, but I thought things needn't change that much, and I retained the name Tess, which lost the D'Urberville connection and was purely related to his testicles. I thought this very apt and appropriate, but it became clear that Tess increasingly resented his name as he developed into a huge, magnificent male cat. I acknowledged to myself and to friends that it was clearly inappropriate to continue with the name – we were both getting funny looks, as he was so obviously male. I reluctantly renamed him Charlie.

Pat Maudsley

Too friendly

We had some friends to stay a few years ago. The husband was not fond of cats, but would never be unkind to them. However, our cat Minnie pushed him to the limit. We had given our bedroom to our friends while my husband and I slept downstairs. Before retiring, I looked for Minnie, but couldn't find her. I thought she had probably crept into one of my sons' rooms, and thought no more about it. When we awoke next morning, she was asleep beside me. Our guests came down to breakfast asking where she was and if she was OK. They then told me where she had been the previous evening. They had gone to bed, having closed the bedroom door. At some point during the night, our friend came to with Minnie sitting on his face! After much thrashing about, his wife managed to catch Minnie and evict her, whilst her husband claimed that his life had been shortened by several years. Needless to say, we made sure we found her each night for the remainder of their stay.

Kim Farrar-Hockley

Party cat

One afternoon while busy in the kitchen, I heard a strange banging noise coming from the back porch. In the porch I found Milly, our tortoiseshell cat, pulling a piece of string through the cat flap. I got down on my hands and knees and looked through the cat flap. There I saw a big pink balloon!

Anonymous

Poorly cat

This is a sad story, but one which is also a source of some amusement. Three years ago I got up one morning to find our lovely ginger cat, Ben, lying under the coffee table. It was winter and I thought he must be cold, so I picked him up and laid him on the sofa, and he purred. I told my mother, who promptly made him a hot water bottle to warm him up. I left for work, giving instructions to keep me informed of how he was. All day I was getting reports that he was not too well and perhaps he should be taken to the vet's. When I got home, Ben was still on the sofa being pampered by my mother with hot water bottles. I rushed in and went to pick him up ready to take to the vet's, but you could have smashed a jeweller's window with him! No hot water bottles would have warmed him up, and that purr he made in the morning must have been his last breath. We didn't know whether to laugh or cry, so we did both. We were very sad, but the vision of my mother fussing over him all day with hot water bottles just makes us laugh.

Jean Thomas

Fenced in

My childhood home was in Durban and we had a kitten named Lovey. During the 1930s, we moved to the Transvaal and my teenage sister's friend kindly adopted our beloved pet. As Gladys called, 'Lovey, Lovey,' the heads of the three youths next door popped up over the fence exclaiming, 'Which one of us do you want?'

Phyllis Thompson

The one that got away

Pushkin Ainsworth, known at the weekend as Mr Pushkin (due to his seniority), was a fabulous companion of ours. Back in the late 1970s, a cat came calling and it was at the time the film *The Cat from Outer Space* was showing and his name was Jake. 'Jake' was with us for about a week, when the local paper had a notice that a ginger tom had gone missing. Jake was reclaimed and it turned out that his owner was Russian and the cat's real name was Pushkin. In 1980 we married and got a cat of our own, calling him Pushkin, after the one that got away.

Kim and Lloyd Ainsworth

Disappearing cat

Our British Red short-haired tabby, Sebastian (Bassi for short), went missing one day in August and didn't reappear for five weeks! We were desperate to find him. He was our children's first pet, and a very affectionate neutered tom. We notified all the local charities and the local vet, and even put up posters where we live. We looked near a local factory and asked the owner if we could check in his outbuildings, but we had no luck. My husband Paul would call for him every night at bedtime in the hope that he might hear and come home. One evening we had a call from the factory owner to say he thought he'd found Bassi. We rushed round and there was Bassi tucking hungrily into a plate of food. He had been crying in a disused lorry, and luckily a woman had heard him and they had broken a window to free him. He had a nasty wound on his neck and was terribly underweight, but after several visits to the vet, and plenty of care at home, he recovered fully and was back to his usual weight. We do rather feel like he tried to use up his nine lives before his second birthday.

Debbie Beard

Sent for the op

Our cat Ginger adopted us ten years ago. He was, as his name suggests, a ginger tom, very masculine and very fond of the ladies – a fact confirmed by the many litters of ginger kittens for miles around. He was actually a stray, but my mother started to put out food for him, and very soon he invited himself in and was regularly found curled up in front of the fire. However, he continued to go out seducing the local population and I decided that if he were going to stay with us, he would have to pay a visit to the vet. At the school where I worked, I was regaling my colleagues in the staff room with Ginger's story saying 'Once he had started eating regularly at our house, I decided he needed to go for the operation.' 'Gosh,' remarked one of the male teachers drily, 'I shall think twice before I come round for tea at your house again!'

Jenni Page

Cat with a fetish

Several years ago we had a cat called Pussy, and every morning in early summer we would come down to one or two very small apples on the kitchen floor. Some mornings there would be quite a few, and this went on through the summer. One morning I came down and I could not see the kitchen floor – it was covered in rotten apples. I was quite relieved when the apple season was over. One evening, my youngest daughter, who was then about eight or nine, was in bed and we heard terrible screaming coming from her, saying that Pussy was running round her room with something bleeding in her mouth. I rushed up there to find Pussy with a strawberry plant in her mouth and a bright red strawberry on it. Pussy obviously had a fruit fetish!

Gay Lander

The hills are alive!

Our first cat was called Whoopee – you can imagine calling him in at night! The best time was when we were staying in Cardingmill Valley, Church Stretton, where we had spent Christmas. Whoopee had gone missing and we had to return home, but my mother-in-law stayed on to find him. She was left wandering the hills, calling out, 'Whoopee!'

Ben Parkes

No bits

After a lot of hunting, we found a lovely tabby she-kitten from the Cats Protection League, so we took her home and called her Tabitha. After a week, I noticed that she didn't breathe very well so we took her to the vet. It cost a lot of money to find out that the poor thing had a deformed chest, which made the heart sit over to one side instead of in the middle, which meant that she only had one usable lung. After any activity, such as play, Tabitha would sit down and look as if she was using her front legs as bellows, trying to get air in. We were warned that Tabitha would not be very fast, would not grow very big and would not make old bones.

After several months and all the inoculations, we took Tabitha to be spayed. I rang later in the day, full of trepidation as the anaesthesia could have spelt the end, and was told that my little girl was now a little boy. We call him Tabbi now and his nickname is Nabbits (as in No Bits!). So far, he has proved the vet wrong; he is very fast and has grown into a big, long-legged cat. But, at the age of nine, he still has to make old bones.

Mandy Payne

Cat in a flap!

Our cat Missy is a little Rex and, bright though she is, she just couldn't get the hang of the cat flap. We spent days pushing her through, first one way, then the other way, to no avail. The door with the cat flap was half-glazed, and one morning Missy was once more pushed through, now in a rather undignified manner, as she had taken to spreading her legs out to try and stop the procedure, but I was determined.

A short while later I sat down at the kitchen table for my coffee and heard a scrabbling at the door. There was Missy, hanging on for dear life peering at me through the glass part of the door. All I could see were enormous ears, eyes and two tiny paws. I opened the door with Missy still clinging to the tiny ledge. She eventually let go and slid down the door very like Tom in a *Tom and Jerry* cartoon. This was always her selected way of making an entrance in future, and shocked many a guest. We have since moved house, and I often wonder what the people who moved in made of the long, deep gouges that were apparent in the back door.

Paula Finney

Exotic names

A few years ago I had two Siamese cats. They were brother and sister and I called them Hoshimoto and Sayonara.

Maureen Jeffs

Kittens galore

A long time ago we had a black female cat called Nebuchadnezzar, or Nebby for short. She was an outdoor cat who only deigned to share our house when she had kittens, which she did twice a year. Then, within a few days, she would be depositing the kittens with our bulldog, Bill, to look after while she went out for a while. We always managed to find homes for the kittens, except for one – a female tabby with enormous feet. We kept her and called her Charlie. Years later there were two Pee Pee's, the first belonging to my mother and the second to me. Pee Pee is short for Phantom Piddler!

Edra Britten

Stylish cats

We acquired two kittens 13 years ago and my youngest son named them Weller (after Paul Weller) and Talbot (after Mike Talbot) of the Style Council band. Unfortunately, Weller is no longer with us, but Talbot is a gorgeous, home-loving cat.

Deirdre Heald

Curtain call

Our cat Millie is a rescue cat from the RSPCA and she is quite a character. She would climb the blinds in the conservatory and jump into the ceiling curtains, thus creating a hammock. To discourage her from doing this, we built a hammock with two washing line props and parasol bases and now she sleeps there, only occasionally making a foray into the curtains.

Joyce and Geoff Raven

Mad Boris

Before my wife and I got married I was privileged to share a part of my life with a grey and white cat whom I named Boris. He came to live with me when he was eight weeks old and I knew at the outset that my life was going to change. He was born at my wife's parents' house in mid-Wales at about the same time that my dog Chloe was born. They had both been rejected by their mothers and so took comfort from each other, to the extent that Boris used to try and suckle from Chloe, and I think he believed he was a dog too. Because of this close relationship, I didn't have the heart to break them up, so Boris came with me as well.

I lived in Kent at the time, so we had quite a journey to make to get home. I felt that Chloe would be fine on the floor on the passenger side of my van, but that Boris, being very tiny and only eight weeks old, would probably be safest and calmer in a well-ventilated cardboard box taped shut with sticky tape. We had the M4 to negotiate, after all, and I didn't want a small cat whizzing about the van for four hours!

Certain that they were both safe, we set off, when after only about two miles there came a terrible tearing noise from behind me. Looking in the rear-view mirror, I could see the top of the box, which was taking on the appearance of a volcano about to blow. From the noises and the growth of the bulge in the top of the box, I knew that something catastrophic was about to happen! Suddenly, after a final ripping sound, Boris's little head popped out of the box, shortly followed by the rest of him. I need not have worried; he enjoyed the journey home. He liked the tassels on my jumper, on which he slept for most of the way but, once it was dark, peering over my right shoulder, what fascinated him most were the car headlights coming towards us. He would spot one coming, concentrate very hard, watching and watching as it got closer and them just as it was about close enough for him to be able to grab it, whoosh! it was gone. Fortunately, there was always another. He loved that game.

Boris was great fun. From the moment I first placed him in the branches of an apple tree, I could see that wide-eyed, self-satisfied look on his face knowing instinctively that this was what he had been born for – just before he fell out of the tree. His face was a picture of surprise when, upon leaping from the kitchen floor onto the draining board, he actually landed in the washing-up water. Then there was the time he leaped onto a table with such gusto that, despite all efforts, he flew straight off the other end, and then pretended that that was exactly what he had intended to do. He even once fell asleep cradled on the top of a clotheshorse where I was drying a sheet in front of the fire. Once the sheet was dry and the friction between the wooden rails and the sheet was gone, Boris, wrapped in the sheet, plummeted to earth, landing with a thud at the bottom!

Years later, when all his chores were done, he would climb on top of our shed and, facing the kitchen window with his paws tucked in, would fall fast asleep. I would say to my wife, 'Boris is at the helm, all is well with the world.'

Roger Birtwhistle

Beauty and the Beast

Several years ago my mother returned home with two female kittens she had found abandoned beside the road. After many days of family deliberations, no one could make a firm decision on names. However, one kitten was far more attractive than the other, and the names Beauty and the Beast soon stuck. Unfortunately, not long after this, Beauty was killed on the road, so we are now left with Beastie, who has grown into a wonderful character and companion.

Neil Whytock

Well utilised

We have an outbuilding-cum-utility room in which we keep the freezer, washing machine and so forth, and our cat Tilly also lives there. We now call it the 'Utilly' room!

Gweneth Collins-Grieve

Natural born killer!

Some years ago I lived near Maidstone with three cats. Two were accomplished hunters, but the third, a tabby and white named Clyde, could never emulate his brothers' exploits no matter how hard he tried. He managed to learn to creep up on birds and mice, but he did it so badly that they always got away before he could spring into action. In desperation, he frequently climbed into a buddleia bush to catch butterflies but, alas, he always crashed to the ground when he lunged forward to grab one.

Some time passed and I was out gardening one day. We backed onto an orchard, which gave the cats plenty of space for recreation. Whilst tending some plants, I heard a peculiar tapping noise and started to look around for the source. I couldn't believe my eyes when I found Clyde, very pleased with himself, bringing back prey for me to see. The prey was a dead grass snake, about 15 inches long. It was so dead, in fact, that it had rigor mortis and it was obviously not Clyde that had killed it. The noise was being caused by Clyde bashing the stiff, horizontal snake against the chestnut paling fence, trying to get it through a short gap!

Allan Robinson

All Greek to me!

I also name my cats from Greek mythology. This all started when I acquired my first Abyssinian. He was called Jason and had belonged to my mother, but came to live with me when she died. I already had a very pretty cat called Stilve. She was named after a racehorse originally. Many years later I found that, like Jason, the name Stilvi also came from Greek mythology, though it's more often written as Stilbe. In fact, in some versions of the myth, Stilvi is the great-great grandmother of Jason. As the two cats had been named completely independently, I thought that this was quite a remarkable coincidence, and resolved that all future cats would be named from the Greek myths. Because I now show and breed Abyssinians, I've probably got through more names than most people. Some of the ones I've used are: Zephyrus, Evander, Phoebus, Leander, Hermione, Calypso, Pandorus and Paris.

Su Startin

Western and Soapy!

Our first cat was a rescue one from Battersea. He is a tall, sleek, black tom who thinks he is far too dignified for such things as playing. We were unable to think of a name for him, as all of our animals over the years have had rather unusual names – so a Fluffy or a Tibbles wouldn't do – when my father, an avid Western fan, came up with the name Randolph. It took us a little while to work out why, until it dawned on us that the vet's receptionist would have to call out 'Randolph Scott.' Our second cat does have an ordinary name – Charlie – as he was a five-year-old rescue cat who had already got used to the name Charlene. Australian soaps have a lot to answer for!

Kerry Scott

Camera-friendly cat

Our poor cat, Tuddy, died recently after a long illness, but he was a real character and during the ten years he was with us he made us laugh a lot. His eating habits were distinctly odd. He loved peas, olives (only green ones and not the stuffed variety!) and honeydew melon. He did eat cat food as well, but never liked milk or cream. Although he was neutered, he seemed to have certain appetites, though not towards female cats, more towards cushions and soft toys! It was very disconcerting when we had visitors, but at least he never tried anything with anyone's trouser leg.

He also had his moments of fame, being a finalist in the Cat World/Whiskas national Pet Cat awards in 1995. He had to tolerate a day-trip drive of over 400 miles to get to the venue. He didn't win, but he also appeared in a Cats Protection League diary and won a CPL photo competition – not bad going for a humble dark ginger and white moggie.

Anne Williams

Little biscuit

We call our furry friend Jaffa Cake, because he's orange, just like the centre of the well-known biscuit.

Bev, Amy and Beatrice

Cat in charge

When our family moved to Manchester during the mid-80s, we acquired a cat – or at least, some responsibilities pertaining to a cat – called Mr Plod. There had been several references to Mr Plod while we were negotiating to buy this particular house in the leafy suburbs of Manchester. We didn't give it much thought at first, as there were other pressing things to arrange, such as schools. But then, Mr Plod loomed on the evening of our moving day. We were spending the night at a local hotel after an exhausting day, packing and transferring the household from Yeovil. We arrived so late that, after a quick look at our new home, we headed for hotel comforts and to get some rest for the following day. Just as we were about to nod off the phone rang, much to our surprise, as nobody knew where we were staying. It was Robert, the previous owner of our house. He was most concerned – had we found the tin of food? Did we remember to feed Mr Plod? We decided he was mad and went to sleep.

Next day we found the food together with instructions for feeding Mr Plod. It seemed that the house really belonged to this animal although so far there was no sign of him. Being responsible parents, we took on this task and put out the food as instructed – outside by an old tea chest in the covered space alongside the garage. The food was eaten and we soon got into the routine. Before long we were rewarded by visits from this rather surly-looking black and white cat. He would pass the kitchen door and give us a stare and disappear. Like most youngsters, our daughter was hoping to form a closer relationship but, despite our best efforts, we never succeeded. Plod would not be picked up and he refused all invitations to cross our threshold – food was OK, but TLC not required! It was a few days later that I was invited to a neighbour's house on some errand and, much to my amazement, there was Mr Plod curled up asleep in front of the fire. 'Oh, yes,' said the neighbour, 'he often comes round for a saucer of milk and a nap.' It turned out that this animal owned the whole block of houses, each of which fulfilled his different needs.

Mike Ottewell

Sweet siblings

We had two cats from the same litter, brother and sister. The male was completely black and the female was tortoiseshell, so we called them Liquorice and Allsorts, although 'Liquorish' was more aptly known as Lick-a-Dish!

Les Hollingbery

Was a what?

Some years back when my three sons were small, we acquired a ginger kitten, whilst they were away visiting grandparents. There was much excitement when they returned home to find a much-wanted new arrival, and their first question was 'What is it?' I said, 'It's a "Was-a" – he's had his operation.' The name stuck and he became Mr Was-a Tom-Cat.

Eileen Anderson

A real fighter

Blackie was as timid as they come, from the Cats Protection League, and it took a whole six months to win him over. Imagine my horror when late last summer I went into the garden to check all was OK, only to hear a tiny miaow. The light was going and I searched for this tiny voice. After much hunting in the undergrowth, I found a very frightened Blackie, picked him up and realised my worst fears – he'd been hit by a car. As we only have two or three cars passing a night, this was one unlucky cat. My wife and I rushed him to the vet's and discovered that his pelvis was broken in five places, there was nothing they could do and only a small chance that he would survive. We spent a sleepless night and the following morning the vet rang to say Blackie was still with us. An obvious fighter, he had crawled 300 yards to the back door to be saved, so all we could do was to love him. Two days later he came home, was placed in a large cage and kept in for six weeks. Little by little his legs came back to full use and he was running around like a kitten again.

The first day we let him out on his own he jumped onto the sheep pen wall and promptly fell off, cutting his side and ending up with a huge scab. He now has a bare patch of skin where the fur never grew back, and we changed his name to Scabby!

Ian

Poor chap!

Nine years ago I lost my beloved Puddy in a road accident, as she had the unfortunate habit of sitting in the middle of the road watching the world go by. I was very upset, so went straight to the local cat sanctuary looking for a fluffy black cat and returned with a tabby and white short-haired cat called BJ. He settled in well and started to show himself as a real character. My mother came to stay soon after his arrival. As only a sprightly 75-year-old mother can, she said: 'Nice cat, dear, what did you say his name was?' 'BJ,' I replied. There was a pause before she replied, 'Bidet, what a stupid name for a cat!' No one could disagree with that, but I could also not continue to call him BJ any more. He immediately became 'Poor little old fella'. Once upon a time it was appropriate, and he always comes when called, so the name has stuck. However, he is not poor, he is enormous in stature, he is far from being old and, owing to the fact that he now belongs to a vet, he is not a fella any more! When we had a cat flap fitted recently, the builder was heard to say, 'That's not a poor little old fella – he has to breathe in just to get through the cat flap!'

Ruth Vernon

Nightmare on Summer Street

For some unknown reason my cat loves to sit on my shoulder, and I thought for a while I was going to call him Long John Silver. However, early one morning I came down to put the kettle on and I was in a state of undress at the time. Unknown to me, the cat was sitting on a work surface behind me and he decided to launch himself through the air to land on my shoulder. Unfortunately, he landed halfway down my back and with four sets of claws, you could hear the scream for miles around as he walked up my back to get onto my shoulder. Hence the name Freddy Kruger. Of course, I always look now when I come down in the mornings!

Philip Griffiths

Musical cat

I got my cat two years after I had finished a music degree, so I wanted to give him a musical name. Eventually, he was named Schubert, usually shortened to Schuby or, by one cruel friend, to Bertie. However, my initial thought was to call him Steinway after the piano, my reason being 'it's the only one I'll ever have'. After only the briefest pause, my brother piped up, 'Perhaps you'd better call him "husband" then.' So cruel, but thus far it seems that he may have been right, as I have neither Steinway nor husband!

Vanessa Hamshere

Nutty biscuit

My sister has a red tabby cat called McVitie because 'he has ginger nuts'! My own cats are called Rufus because he's red; Fergus, because he's very furry; and Millie, whom we acquired on New Year's Eve 1999 and promptly called her The Millennium Moggie.

Diane Read

Nota bene

One of our cats is called NB. Before he came to live with us, no matter how much we racked our brains, we couldn't come up with a suitable name. I suggested that, as a working name until we could think of something more appropriate, we should call him NB – short for New Baby. Being an extremely lazy couple, we never did get round to finding a 'proper' name, so NB he has remained to this day, although it now means Naughty Boy!

Michael Garrett

Nervous habit

We have had two cats for some 13 years, named Issy and Pooh. Issy was named after my hero, Isambard Kingdom Brunel and has turned out to be a bit of a wimp, not at all suited to his name. Pooh was christened Poppy originally, as she had a very pretty sunburst face. However, as a kitten, she

Above:
*Proud new
parents – what
shall we call him?*

Left:
*At least we match
the decor.*

Right:
*I'm practising my
most penetrating
stare for when I'm
grown up... SK
says IF you EVER
grow up!*

Above:

Pegguy with kittens Impey, Muzzy, Izzet and Robbie (Savage) (p. 12).

Contributor: Moira Baker

Right:

Robbie Savage, staking his claim on the food bowl (p. 12).

Contributor: Moira Baker

Above:
Three unknown poseurs, snapped atop a dustbin lid. (p. 108).
Contributor: Brian Batty

Left:
Felix Box in snooze mode (p. 103).
Contributors: Jennie and Lee Robertson

Clockwise from right:

Otis trying to 'catch' the Thanksgiving turkey (p. 103).
Contributor: Sue Cox

Millie, in her specially made hammock (p. 77).
Contributors: Joyce and Geoff Raven

Mushka in her favourite place – the inside of a tissue box! (p. 21).
Contributor: Anne Bedford

Chenna helping the postman (p. 104).
Contributor: Helen M. Hayes

Opposite:
*Misty, looking
as appealing as
possible!* (p. 106).
Contributor:
Dawn Rendell

Left:
*Cariad, keeping
the keys warm.*
(p. 108).
Contributor:
Robert J. Nash

Below:
*Susie, 'monitoring'
the heat.* (p. 108).
Contributor:
Robert J. Nash

Above:

Just wait till the winter snows and I'll come into my own!

Right:

Sarah Kennedy and Andy Sparkes, a vet at the Animal Health Trust, share a word with an anonymous moggie.

was extremely nervous and if anyone picked her up, she responded with an emission of foul-smelling air from the tail end. Most people responded to this by uttering 'Poo!' Hence, her name changed to Pooh.

Terry and Catherine Bennett

Tipsy road

Years ago I got two white kittens from the Cats Protection League. Trying to find original names for them, we came up with Moselle and Chablis. The idea of having white cats was that, as I was losing my sight, I thought they would show up more. When I took them for their initial visit to the vet, he remarked on the fact that it seemed that our road was obsessed with alcohol. The vicar had two cats named Newcastle and Brown and another neighbour had a cat called Brandy. I feel so pleased that I was able to enjoy my 'wines'.

Audrey Butler

A complete mishmash

Our two cats are called Mish and Mash. We got them from the RSPCA and the male cat didn't have a clue what his name was. The female knew hers as Rubbish. We realised that she only looked up when she heard the 'sh' sound, so we decided on Mish and as a pair he became Mash.

Richard Copper

'Help-yourself Herbie'

We have shared our home with many wonderful cats over the years, but one of the most characterful cats was Herbert, or Herbie Cat. He would make friends with anyone and often we were told he went for walks across the surrounding fields with anyone he met. Once we had goldfish deposited on the lawn and a neighbour commented that there must be a heron in the area – had we seen one near his pond? One Sunday lunchtime, we were aware of Herbie eating something at the far end of the garden. When I went to investigate what poor creature had given its life, I realised that Herbie had a complete and freshly cooked chicken leg. To this day, we have no idea where it came from, but then Herbie had a habit of wandering in and out of houses and was known to help himself!

John and Teresa Southall

A cunning plan

We acquired a ten-week-old stray kitten, a most beautiful tabby with a truly magnificent tail just like a Christmas tree. He arrived riddled with fleas and worms, so the obvious name had to be Baldrick. He was a superb cat who thought he was a dog and bonded with our big male 'lassie' dog – the pair of them were inseparable. However, Baldrick never forgot his humble beginnings. He had a habit of bringing in earthworms dangling from his mouth and then depositing them on the lounge floor.

Sheila Stickells

Purr-fect

We had three cats in the 70s and 80s. One was named Chaucer, for no particular reason and the second was called Yum-Yum. The third one had a very loud purr and was therefore named Perdita.

E. Marriott

Hectoring Hector

We think Hector is an excellent name for a cat and chose it for one of ours. He is an enormous tabby and looks very brave and fierce, like his Greek namesake. In fact, he is a wimp and is terrified of the two much smaller females in our family. His voice is light and soft and not the roar you would expect from a Greek hero! We got Hector from a rescue centre and he was difficult to begin with. We kept him in for the recommended two weeks, during which time he destroyed most of my curtains in his futile attempts to get out of the windows. Now he is the most loveable cat you could imagine, although he has a nasty habit of bringing live mice into the house and letting them go!

Jill Thynne

Chemical cats

When my cat had her first litter of kittens, my sister happened to be learning the periodic table. For that reason, the kittens were tagged Hydrogen, Helium, Lithium, Beryllium and Boron – all easily identifiable by being pure white, apart from little black spots on their heads. Unfortunately, the last one out, Boron, was the runt and became known as Boron the Moron. However, he went to live with my cousin and became Beanly Blue, after a type of cheese!

Patricia Singleton

Rebel cat

A cousin of mine, whilst experiencing his rebellious teenage years, named his cat Trotsky!

Ian and Ken

Old gent

My cat, Mr Purrkins, is a portly, one-eyed, elderly, black furry gent with a white shirtfront and paws.

Gill Robinson

Ratty cat

Ginger Bits is from the Cats Protection League and I got her as I needed a cat to have words with the rats at the stable yard where I kept my horses. Unfortunately, it has transpired that Bits has no teeth at all, so all she could really have done, on being presented with a rat, was gum it to death! As her days as a ratter were long gone, I brought her home and she now spends her time eating, sleeping and beating up our Rottweiler puppy.

Lucy Kerrigan

Fly me, I'm Sprocket!

My parents named their new kitten Sprocket. It was very lively and would play with bits of string until it literally dropped from exhaustion. Last summer when it was still a very small and light kitten, it was practising hunting in the back garden. My mother was washing up in the kitchen and could see the whole garden. In particular, she could see a large wood pigeon hopping around on the grass. What happened next defies belief. The kitten emerged at high speed from the bushes and made straight for the pigeon.

The pigeon, sensing the cat approaching, tried to take off, but not before the kitten sank his teeth into its tail. Amazingly, because the kitten was so light, both cat and bird became airborne and started to gain altitude! When they got to about six or eight feet with the kitten still hanging on, the pigeon lost its balance and they fell to the ground. Luckily, the kitten was temporarily stunned by this and let go. Sprocket then chased the pigeon all the way across the lawn until they reached the fence, at which point the pigeon was just high enough to escape. This escapade left pigeon feathers all over the lawn and the kitten was unbearably smug for the next few days.

Peter Spikings

Avenging cat

My estranged wife's cat is called Purdy, originally after the character in *The Avengers*, but I think it suits the makers of the shotguns better, as she too can kill from close range. She nearly took my leg off one night trying to climb on the bed when I had the covers pulled back, and although she is about 15, her paws are still like lightning.

Barry Trump

Timid and hungry

Our cats are called Timmy and Kitkat. Timmy was very timid when we first got him and Kitkat loves chocolate. Timmy went missing for four nights about a year ago. It turned out that he was locked in a neighbour's conservatory and since he returned home, he's been permanently hungry – he could eat for England! He's also very fond of hot, buttered crumpets. He still partly retains his timid side as he loves to chase butterflies, but when he catches them he hasn't a clue what to do with them.

Zena and Andy Morris

In flagrante delicto!

Cougar is named after John Cougar Mellencamp (the rock guitarist) and is missing a front leg following a suicidal leap from an upstairs window as a kitten. Fortunately, he doesn't seem any worse off for his loss. However, since his second visit to the vet involving another (more personal) amputation, he has become generally anti-social. Having grown up in the middle of Leicester, Cougar's favourite food is curry and he will happily chomp on raw green chillies as a snack.

Cosmic, my lovely black moggie, moved in following his owner's abrupt departure from the neighbourhood. He waits for the car when I come home from work and we've trained him to say 'ham' in request for his favourite snack.

Finally, Tigerlily (Lily or Lil for short) is my champion mouser, who regularly goes missing for a week and returns triumphant with some poor creature or other. The largest so far has been a weasel, which I found wrapped around the leg of the dining table, and the most unusual probably a snake. When she can't find any live prey she brings me other people's cat toys as compensation. She has a boyfriend, Jack 'The Cat' McVitie from next door. I once found them actively enjoying each other's company on my bed (despite Lily having been seen to) and was so embarrassed that I muttered, 'Sorry,' backed out of the room and left them to it!

Elizabeth Follenfant

Toilet trouble

My daughter Tracy has two cats named Bronte and Darcy. Both are as mad as each other, but neither seems to learn from the other's mistakes. For example, one morning Tracy was rudely awoken by a commotion in the bathroom and then the sound of paws running very fast along the hall into the lounge. Upon further investigation, it became apparent that Darcy had fallen into the toilet. Only two days later Tracy herself was in the bathroom when Bronte decided that she wanted to have a look at the thing that had caused poor Darcy so much distress. And headfirst into the toilet she went! However, not being as slim as Darcy, Bronte couldn't get herself out and, after much flailing of paws, Tracy grabbed her by the tail and pulled her out. Scampering away, she wasn't to be seen for at least half an hour, obviously hiding her embarrassment and waiting to dry off. However, in true cat style she was very snooty towards Tracy afterwards, as if she was appalled that she had dared to grab her by the tail. How very undignified!

June Rylance

There's a tiger in my tank!

Having arrived at our apartment in Spain, the first thing to do was to go to the supermarket to stock up with food. I got the car out of the garage and left it for a few minutes 'ticking over' outside the apartment. My sister and I set out for our usual journey, but after a while we could hear miaowing. We stopped, checked inside the car, opened the boot and even checked the exhaust pipe. Thinking we had both lost our marbles, we continued our journey but could still hear a cat. I stopped again. This time my sister detected it was coming from under the bonnet. Up went the bonnet and we found a cat lying on the engine. How it got there is a mystery, but we grabbed it and returned home without any shopping!

Freda Buttle

Rockin' cats

Some years ago I used to engrave cat and dog identity tags as part of my work. One day a lady asked me to engrave tags for her two cats. One cat was called Bebop and the other was called Alula. When I mentioned what unusual names they were, she said she had called them those names so that she could stand on the back doorstep and sing out Bebop-Alula when calling them in!

Jim

Heathcliffe, come home!

Our kitten, Heathcliffe, went missing one day, just after I had closed the washing machine door and switched it on. After a search of the house and garden, I looked with trepidation in the direction of the washing machine. Surely he couldn't be in there? I switched it off immediately and, being very squeamish, flew round to my parents who lived next door, pouring out my tale of woe. We rushed back to my kitchen, where we frantically tried to open the door, but to no avail. My mother peered through the porthole and screamed, 'I can see an ear!' We were desperate and very upset. My father was still making vain attempts to open the door, when suddenly, in through the kitchen door walked Heathcliffe, with all the poise and petulance of a ten-week-old kitten. Heathcliffe departed this life last year, and we were all very sad to lose him at only ten years old, but his best friend, Louis Armstrong, is still with us. I adore cats and really admire their 'You didn't choose me, I chose you' attitude. All we really get to choose are their names!

Wendy Lewis

Size isn't everything!

My two little angels Frank and Georgia were taken to the vet's to be neutered and spayed. How embarrassed was I when the vet told me that my pretty little Georgia was indeed a George? 'Are you sure?' I questioned. 'But you could see he was a boy,' replied the vet. 'Well, he was nowhere near as well-endowed as Frank!' I said in my defence.

Lesley Weeks

Breakfast cat

My cat is called Pudding, not because she is fat, but because she is all black – black pudding! It is a dish that is definitely not on the menu in our house!

Rachel Eyre

Matching pair

We used to run a pub in rural Oxfordshire, so when two stray kittens appeared on our doorstep we named them Gin and Tonic. On a visit to the vet's, the assistant came out and asked, 'Who's next – Gin and Tonic, or Thatcher and Kinnock?' We all thought they went together very well.

Jane Clifford

Puny no more

An old boss of mine called his cat Mr Puniverse. It arrived as a very bedraggled, skinny kitten at the vet's surgery where his wife worked. The kitten was duly adopted, christened and fed until it became an extremely large, long-haired, ginger tom-cat which belied its origins.

Heather Lunnon

Biker cats

A friend of a friend named her new kitten Moped. This was because she ascertained that the kitten's father was a cat down the road named Kawasaki!

Andrew White

Catcall

We heard the neighbours whose house abutted onto ours at the end of their garden calling their cat in each night – 'Toothpaste, Toothpaste.' We thought it strange, had a giggle and forgot about it. When we got to know them many weeks later, we found out that the cat was named Topaz.

Marion Heron

Chairman of the board

We have a number of cats managing our household. The present management committee consists of four, and I always wait a little while before naming them so I can see how their characters develop. The present incumbents include two ginger tabby girls, one called Gizmo because she was the runt of the litter and had huge ears. Needless to say, she has grown into and surpassed her ears to become a very rotund cat. Her sister, Yoda, also had large ears but is possessed of a more ethereal quality. Regrettably, she has none of the wisdom of the original Yoda and must be looked upon as the airhead of the cat world.

Our third little lady is Marmite, a dark brown tortoiseshell, and certainly no lady! Marmite seemed to suit her colouring and also her temperament as she was in a bit of a pickle when she came to us, and it has taken six years for her to learn to play and enjoy a cuddle and a tickle behind the ears. The last of our committee and present chairman came to us three years ago. He is a blue-eyed, snow-spotted Bengal and very handsome. He is also very intelligent and has worked out how to open all the doors in the house. His current work-in-progress is the new patio door. When he arrived, he looked so sweet. He would cuddle up to Gizmo treating her as his surrogate mother, and the two of them looked adorable. His pedigree name was Mafdet Snowspangle and I toyed with many names on an ice and snow theme. However, within a couple of weeks, his true character started to emerge. One day, when within the space of a few hours he had terrorised the older cats yet again, tried to climb the garage wall, yet again, in order to pick a fight with one of the local tom-cats, and had tried to follow next door's tom through his own cat flap to show him who was boss, despite there being three dogs on the other side . . . it came to me. There was only one thing to call him: Sodric, because he is such a little sod!

Barbara and Gareth Jones

Common as muck?

My first cat, a large, Siamese chocolate point, was bought for me as a present by my parents and sister. Before I was to pick him up, my sister Vivien called me and said that she had to register his name urgently (I now know this was not the case!). Alan and I had been thinking of grand names for this grand cat and hadn't come to a decision, but I told her to register him as Tutankhamen. She called back a couple of days later and said the name had been registered and it was Tooting Common, wasn't it?

Well, the name stuck, even though I do know better not to be so naïve now! A couple of years later we decided to get Tooting a brother and, keeping in line with the 'common' theme, we called him Wandsworth.

Fiona

Thoughtful cat

We always knew we had a highly intelligent pet in Worcester, our beautiful 15-year-old black cat. He regularly opens doors by the handle, scoops food out of his bowl with his paw and is very vocal in getting his point across. However, he is also very generous and has often brought us some strange gifts over the years. One recent gift that springs to mind is the small mouse that he brought home and deposited proudly on the doorstep. The effort of catching mice for an old chap like Worcester is now a little too much, as in this particular instance, the mouse was delivered held in the mouth by the tail, complete with wooden mousetrap attached! Well, it's the thought that counts, isn't it?

Viv and Col

Thieving cat

When my Mum was single she had a cat called Snoopy who, in the prime of his life, was very agile and would catch anything that moved. At the end of Mum's garden was a stream and Snoopy would bring presents of birds and mice, as most cats do. However, she then discovered that if she sat in the water she could catch frogs and take them into the kitchen, where they would jump around. This was not too bad, but when Snoopy brought home a full-sized parrot, things started to get serious. This parrot was followed a week later by yet another! At the time, these parrots were worth about £100 each, which was more money than my Mum could afford. To top it off, Snoopy brought home a neighbour's fully grown chicken. The squawking bird was not dead, but running around with large bald patches. When the neighbour came round and said, 'Your cat's got my chicken,' Mum denied all knowledge, and then noticed she was standing in a pile of chicken feathers!

Emma

Distress signal?

My colleague Glenn Miller (who has never forgiven his parents for christening him Glenn) was given a pedigree male Burmese cat by his partner Sarah, for his birthday. Glenn's mind having been warped by constant quips about his own name, he wanted to find the most inappropriate name possible for the unfortunate cat. He therefore named it Foghorn Leghorn, after the cartoon chicken. This soon became shortened to just Foghorn.

A couple of years later, they decided to get a female Siamese kitten, as they had been told that a Burmese/Siamese cross produces a very attractive cat. Again came the problem of finding an appropriate name for the new kitten. They eventually came up with Siren as a name for Foghorn's new friend.

Andrew Grasemann

Dangerous game

I used to live in Camps Bay in Cape Town on the mountain side, with two Siamese cats, Princess Sushi and Mr Sam. Their favourite trick was to catch a mountain scorpion and bring it into the house. Then they would play a game with it, each cat tapping the scorpion and trying to avoid its stinging tail. Once they had finished playing, Mr Sam would pick up the scorpion, drop it in the dog's water bowl where the exhausted creature would drown, and the two cats would retire to a nice cosy bed for a sleep after their exciting game. Not so impressed was my dog, with a strange thing floating in her water bowl.

John

Cat-apult

There is a very funny cat story that was reported in the *Fortean Times* about three years ago, and it purports to be true. It was apparently taken from the *Bournemouth Evening Echo* and I still fall about laughing every time I think of it. A vicar was trying to retrieve his cat from a tall tree in his front garden. The hapless animal kept climbing upwards, miaowing desperately, despite all the vicar's efforts to lure it down. He hit on the grand plan to urge it downwards by lassoing the branch it was on and tying it to the bumper of his car, hoping it would follow the downward tilt of the branch. As this didn't help, he decided to drive his car slowly away from the tree, to draw the branch down even further. The car crept slowly away from the tree until, with a resounding snap, the rope broke and the branch sprang skyward, hurling the unsuspecting moggie into space. Meanwhile, a couple of roads away, a little girl was enjoying a picnic with her mother in their back garden. 'Mummy, please can we have a pussy cat?' pleaded the little girl. 'Well, dear,' said the mother, piously, 'we'll have to ask God about that.' At that moment, the unfortunate airborne feline plummeted onto their lawn. Needless to say, it has remained with the little girl ever since!

Maggie Lomax

Double escape

In the mid-70s I was banqueting manager at the Adelphi Hotel in Liverpool. Having decided to get a cat, I went off to the local cat and dog home one day. Inspecting the rows of cages of available moggies, purring and pawing at the front of their cages, desperate to be chosen, I became aware of one particular cat. Obviously older than the others, he sat disdainfully at the back of his cage. On enquiring, I was told that it was his last day in the home before the big needle. He was half-Persian, half-moggie, had no known history and no name. I took him and he reluctantly agreed and we set off to my flat and huge overgrown garden.

The next day, I went to work leaving the cat in the garden. On returning I couldn't find him anywhere and, fearing that he had run off, checked the jungle of a garden anyway. I found him lying in obvious pain with his paws in the air near the back wall and, gently picking him up, took him to the local vet. He was examined and X-rayed and I was told he had broken his pelvis in what must have been a fall off the wall. The vet said it would probably be better to have him put down there and then, as convalescence would be long and tricky; but I decided that, having come this far, I would give it a try and gave consent for his operation to proceed. When the vet asked for the cat's name, I said 'Pelvis, of course!'

The operation was a success and I collected a woozy Pelvis a couple of days later. It wasn't easy trying to keep a cat sedentary for a fortnight and he used to go to work with me, and spend his day in the telephonists' room until I had finished. Now known by all as Pele, he made a full recovery and became a fiercely loyal but very independent cat that no self-respecting dog would ever dare approach. When I moved to London, Pele went to stay with my parents in the Borders, terrorising all animal life there until he died at the ripe old age of 20 – not bad for a homeless moggie who twice faced the needle in the space of two days nearly 19 years earlier.

Douglas Newlands

Lucky dip!

One day when I was about 10 years old, Mum and I were sitting by the garden pond, enjoying the sunshine. Suddenly, a yowling grey ball appeared over the high fence and plummeted straight into the water. As we recovered from the shock, we heard some youths running away, laughing. Looking back to the pond, we saw that the grey ball was actually a small and very frightened kitten. My Mum fished her out (no goldfish missing!) and we took her inside. A little while later, milk and hairdryer applied, the loveliest kitten appeared. She had almost a Burmese Blue look about her, but most of all she was very cute. For some time, Mum tried to find out if she belonged to anyone, but nobody came forward. It seemed that we had found a cat – or she had found us!

It was time to choose a name. We eventually picked Lucky,

because we thought she'd had a lucky dip in our pond. Little did we know that we were the lucky ones. She was a tremendous pet for many years.

Jean Livingstone

Opera or comedy?

I have a cat called Pavarotti. He is a large, fat tabby cat with the loiudest cry I have ever heard from a cat. My other two cats are called Nanu Nanu and Shazbat – my ex-husband was a *Mork and Mindy* fan!

Gillian Gundry

Literary connection

Our two cats are called Horatio and Tobermory. Horatio is named after Nelson, with whom one of my ancestors sailed. In fact, he is well named because he has a fascination for water and likes to walk round the bath with a nautical air.

Tobermory is named, not after the Womble or the capital of the Isle of Mull, but after the talking cat of the same name in the *Tales of Saki* by H.H. Munro. This literary Tobermory used to hide under chairs, listen in to conversations and report back to the owners on what he'd heard. Our Tobermory is a blue cream tortoiseshell and came to us from an animal rescue centre 16 years ago, having been thrown over a wall with fireworks tied to her. I'm pleased to say she is now a happy, contented cat.

Harry and Linda Sutton

Nice but dim

Our current cat is called Hazel, after the chief rabbit in *Watership Down*. She is a great cat, but not very bright. She cherishes the idea that she is a mighty hunter but, fortunately, she's not. We get a lot of parrots coming to feed on our bird table (we live in Australia), which is screwed to the rail of our balcony. Last time Hazel fancied parrot for tea she eyed up her target, bunched up her hindquarters and sprang, only to miss the parrot completely and go sailing over the rail to land in the garden 20 feet below! She tried to pretend that it was part of her plan, but I knew better.

Neil the Pom

Snap happy

Our daughter, Sarah, lives in Atlanta, Georgia. She and her husband Hugh have a very cheeky cat called Otis, who just can't resist trying to reach food that is not strictly meant for him! Last year we visited them for Thanksgiving and managed to get a highly entertaining picture of Otis trying to 'catch' the Thanksgiving turkey. We are going again this year and will have our camera at the ready!

Sue Cox

Dot.com cat

Felix Box is now eight years old. His name comes from the fact that, as a kitten, he adored boxes, or any secluded space, and still does. His love of boxes has meant that, on occasion, Felix has gone missing a few times. One day, as a young kitten, he managed to get shut in a cupboard for the whole morning, sending the household into frantic searches. Once found, he then sauntered into the cupboard under the stairs and got shut in all afternoon! Currently, he has taken up residence under a kitchen cupboard, as he hates fireworks.

Next is Febe-Ivy Ginger Bits, who is five. She is small, neat and beautiful and can scrap with the best of them. Febe is a rescue cat and lived rough for her first few weeks – we assume this is where she learnt her 'scrapping' skills. As a tiny kitten first let loose in the garden, she would always hide in the overgrown ivy and was very difficult to coax out. The rest of her name explains her unusual tortoiseshell coat.

Last but not least is our youngest cat (18 months) called Sandi Claws.com. He's big, he's brave and he's ginger! Sandi suited him as a kitten, but he just kept growing and growing. The 'Claws' bit gives him street-cred, but the '.com' is his very own as, over one ear he has a small, pale, ginger dot!

Jennie and Lee Robertson

Helping postie

My cat is a beautiful little tabby called Chenna. When I was a very small girl, my mother used to name my dolls and one in particular was called Suzanna. However, my attempt to pronounce the name came out as 'Shenna' and it stuck. My mother always loved the name and when I was older asked if I would consider it as a name if I had a daughter myself. My mother died 16 years ago and I never did have any children, but when the time came to name my kitten, Shenna came back to me. When I told my partner, he would hear of no other name and we changed the spelling to Chenna. She likes to help out the postman by jumping up at the door to grasp in her mouth any letters or newspaper coming through the letterbox.

Helen M. Hayes

Mousetrap

Shelly was a beautiful tortoiseshell cat who was friendly, amusing and very communicative. She lived next door with our neighbours who, living in the country, kept a cat to keep the mice at bay. Shelly did this very well, not only for our neighbours, but also for us, as she considered both houses her home. One day, some 12 years ago, I became uneasy that I hadn't seen Shelly for a few days. Later on, while working in the kitchen, I was more than a little unnerved by a mouse, which jumped out of the toaster! This heightened my unease about Shelly's whereabouts and my shrieks of horror brought my husband, Jim, into the house. He had just been talking to a passer-by who had seen a tortoiseshell cat caught in a gin trap further up the lane. Jim and our neighbour Ruth went to investigate and found poor Shelly by the side of the lane, having dragged herself and the trap through a field. The vet patched her up wonderfully and put her leg in a cast for a while. Perhaps because Jim held Shelly on the trip to the vet, a bond was created between them. The next day a tapping at the back door turned out to be Shelly 'pawing' the door with her cast asking to be let in.

So, was it coincidence that, in 17 years, the only mouse we have seen in our house was when Shelly was caught in a trap?

Jenny Dahms

Swinging cat

When my daughter Victoria was eight, she was desperate for a kitten. We tried to persuade her otherwise, but one day her Dad gave in and she and I went to look for a kitten. We returned an hour later with a six-week-old Siamese blue point called Chu Che Ameratto. He joined our family of two German Shepherds, Kayleigh and Major (both females) and Betsy Brown, a Heinz 57. As the only male, he quickly took charge and flew from one place to another via the TV, the top of the kitchen cupboards, halfway up the curtains and the tops of doors, to name just a few places. He achieved an NVQ in lighting by swinging on the wall switches to turn them on and off, and Olympic-style agility was displayed when he would knock the handset off the phone each time it rang! Consequently, my daughter named this blue-eyed boy Fly, or Mr Fly when he was very naughty. Soon Mr Fly began to think he was a dog and would run to the door whenever the doorbell rang! He was very vocal and had a large vocabulary, not to mention an annoying habit of sleeping with whoever was available, purring all night with his nose on one's cheek!

Jane Freda

From stray to spoilt cat!

Our beautiful Tiger had a very ignominious beginning. He was a stray who turned up one day in our garden, pitiful, smelly, half-dead and starving. You could see the bones sticking through his skin, he was so thin. When he saw me he hid, but I put food out for him and, after two months of this, he decided to stay. He now spends most of his days snoozing and dreaming, being fed on fish, chicken and the cream from the top of the milk. He seems to love his new family, especially the grandchildren.

Yvonne Clark

Pretty kitty

Our much-loved kitten, now four months old, is very beautiful and has long soft grey fur, hence the name Misty. She is full of mischief, but fortunately gets on well with Tiggy, a six-year-old ginger male and Rufus, our 13-year-old apricot poodle.

Dawn Rendell

On Ilkley Moor bar cat!

I named my cat Ilkley, because my surname is Moore! He has a brother called Bodmin.

Maureen Moore

Gang of boys

I have a 'gang' of cats, all boys and all with very different personalities. Jaffa is a large ginger and white gentleman, whose favourite day is dustbin day. He likes to investigate all the rubbish bags waiting for the dustcart. He also likes window-cleaning day, when he takes himself up the ladder, sometimes as far as the roof, and waits up there until our long-suffering window cleaner carefully carries him down on his shoulders!

The next one is Pippin, a home-loving boy who likes to spend lots of time in a fleecy radiator hammock. He is very fond of his food and lurks in waiting until the other two have finished and then he has a good tidy-up. If he can, he will steal a large mouthful of their food and then rush back to his own bowl to eat it, so that nobody will know! The only thing that gives him away is that he growls at the stolen goods.

Last is Wilfred White. He is definitely the most mischievous, but adorable little chap you could ever meet. He has a large black spider friend with pipe cleaner legs and often takes it to look out of the window with him. His best friend of all is Lucy, our eight-year-old boxer dog, and they love to play together – usually in the middle of the sitting-room floor when we have guests.

Julia Moule

The warmest spot

Isn't it funny how cats always find the warmest spot to sit? Our cat Cariad (Cari for short) often sits on top of my computer keyboard. This, as you can imagine, has had a few unusual effects on my computer, and Cari often looks at me as if to say, 'Where is that beeping noise coming from? I'm just keeping the keys warm for you.' Our other cat is called Susie, and she has an unerring talent for finding the warmest spot. She is often to be found sleeping on top of my wife, Sandra's, monitor!

Robert J. Nash

Hopalong

My son Steve has a cat called Cassie. She is missing her back left leg, as she was mauled by a dog when she was a kitten. Steve found her in an RSPCA cattery and it was love at first sight. The first name he came up with was Tripod, but this was discounted in favour of Hopalong Cassidy – Cassie for short. Sometimes she thinks she's a fur hat or collar, as she loves to drape herself around Steve's head and neck. Despite her disability and age (she is 12), she still climbs onto the pitched garage roof, torments the dog across the road, and leaves balls of fur (not her own!) blowing in the wind when defending her territory from other cats.

Bernice Mee

Snapped

I used to live in Surbiton, Surrey. One day in 1984 I was just reversing my car into the drive, when I caught sight of three cats who looked like they were posing especially for the camera. I always carry a camera with me and managed to get a shot of them, sitting snuggled up together on a dustbin lid, before they took off. I never knew their names, but I was thrilled to get such a good picture.

Brian Batty

Mistaken identity

My cats, Willow and Catkin, are brother and sister, now aged nine. The local dog warden found them, tied up in a sack in a builder's skip. Luckily, she heard them and rescued them before any more bricks and rubble were thrown on top. She already had numerous animals and 13 cats, so she brought the kittens to me. At that time I had a rough collie and I wasn't sure how they would get on, but thankfully they all got along fine. Then one morning, the postman knocked to say that Catkin was lying in the road, having been knocked over. I looked down the road and could see this little cat, but couldn't bring myself to go and look close up in case he was badly mangled. The phone was ringing, so I went indoors to answer it and it was a friend, whom I told about Catkin. She very kindly said her husband would come and fetch Catkin and bury him in their large orchard. This was duly done.

To my great surprise, at lunchtime Catkin came walking up the garden path – I had buried someone else's cat! I did not think there would be two identical grey cats in the area and, needless to say, the owners were not amused when I told them I had buried their cat.

Rosemary Beckford

Ambitious hunter

Oscar was the best cat in the world, a tall tabby with a gammy leg (from an accident in his youth). He came to live with me because he didn't like the Alsatian dog at his house, who used to carry him around and wash him as if he was a puppy! As we had a cat flap, Oscar just moved in. He was the most affectionate and lovable cat, but also the most agile hunter. The house was always full of dead rabbits (half-eaten) or dead rats, and the lounge carpet never recovered, often looking as if some horrific chainsaw massacre had taken place. On one memorable occasion, Oscar tried to get a large wood pigeon through the cat flap. Luckily, it wouldn't fit, and when I opened the back door there was an enormous pile of feathers and the dead bird with wings outspread – not a pleasant sight first thing in the morning! Another time, he came into the back garden with a moorhen in his mouth, its legs dangling piteously. Happily for this bird, my husband rescued it and sent it on its way back to the village pond. Sadly Oscar got run over on one of his hunting trips across the road to the fields, but I always think cats choose who they live with and one day another cat may turn up on my doorstep.

Linda Poynter

Strange quartet

Our cats have rather strange names. Resident in our household, we have Tanith and Taegus, named after Carthaginian deities, Nimrod, named after the hunter and Nitten, who is the kitten of the family.

Roger Sturgeon

Uninvited guest

It was one of those all-too-rare sunny Sundays when the barbecue had behaved itself; the grown-up children had gone their separate ways with their partners and my wife Jenny and I could relax – me in the garden by the pond with a glass of wine and Jenny napping in the shade of the lounge. The silence was broken by a shout from inside and, as I looked round, a small tabby cat emerged from the French windows quickly followed by Jenny asking 'Where did you come from?' It would appear that the cat had entered the house via the open kitchen door and as Jenny woke from her nap she was astonished to see our uninvited guest strolling through the lounge and out onto the patio as though she lived there. She immediately charmed us by rolling on her back and 'chirping' (there's no other way I can describe the sound she made). She was wearing a red collar but no form of identification. Our pond and goldfish soon became her centre of attention and by the time we were ready to turn in for the night, she was showing no signs of wanting to go home. We locked up for the night with her outside and assumed that she must be local and would find her way home.

Imagine our surprise the next morning when we opened the front door to find her outside – but not for long. In she came and of course, we had to find her something to eat – tinned tuna was the only suitable thing, and remains her favourite treat. She stayed around the house all day and by this time we realised she wasn't going anywhere if she had the choice. She appeared to be in excellent condition and had a large patch of newly grown fur, indicating recent surgery. We contacted the local vet and arranged for her to be examined to see if they had done the surgery and could identify her. They didn't know her, but proclaimed her to be in good health. She settled in to her new abode and we waited anxiously for the local newspaper to see if anybody had placed a 'Lost' advert for her. The paper duly arrived and there was no advert. We were relieved and pleased that we could keep her. However, our more observant daughter Katie phoned us, having spotted an advert that described the cat perfectly. I rang the number and it transpired that the cat had come from a local rescue centre to join a household which already had one cat. She had only been there two days when she decided that it wasn't big enough for both of them. Remarkably, they lived no more than 50 yards away in the row of houses that back onto ours. They came round to see us and saw how quickly she had settled in. They told us that, although less than 12 months old, she had already had kittens and been abandoned by her first owners. The rescue centre had taken her in and she had then helped feed orphaned kittens before being spayed and found a new home. They could see how contented she was, and as we had now had her longer than they had, agreed that she could stay if we wanted her. By this time we would have been devastated to lose her and so she was officially our cat.

She spent the first few weeks in our house snooping into every room, getting into cupboards, wardrobes and drawers and seemed to be searching for something, maybe her own kittens. Thus she became Snoopy, and is the most good-natured cat I have ever come across, even charming non-cat people!

Geoff Walters

The dead cat test

This is a true story. A kindergarten pupil told his teacher that he had found a cat. She asked if it was dead or alive. 'Dead,' she was informed. 'How do you know?' she asked. 'Because I pissed in his ear and he didn't move,' said the child, innocently. 'You did what!' exclaimed the teacher, in shock. 'You know,' explained the boy, 'I leaned over and went "Pssst" and he didn't move.'

Gordon Urquhart

Music appreciation

In the 1960s when my children were small, a friend bought my daughter Geraldine a pretty little all-black, half-Persian kitten for her eighth birthday. We decided to name him Count Pizzicato (a musical term). I believe there was a TV programme in the 1950s with a cat of that name. He grew into the most beautiful cat and my husband told me it was my fault the cat was such a snob, because I was always telling him he was a handsome Italian man! He just hated *Top of the Pops* on TV, and would run out of the room when the children wanted to watch it. But on Sundays, he loved to watch *Songs of Praise* and would sit about four inches from the TV screen absolutely enthralled and obviously drinking in the music. It still makes us laugh now and we talk about 'The Count', as my husband called him, with great affection.

Abina Smith

Chapel cats

When we retired to the Cotswolds, we were lucky enough to find on the market a converted Methodist chapel. In looking for suitable feline company (with mouser potential), we decided that colouring of a demure black would be appropriate, preferably with two white tabs below the chin. A local farm was offering twin kittens, a male, all in black, and his sister, also in black but with white socks and shirtfront. We were enchanted and took them home, discussing with what names they should be christened. It didn't take long, for they were carried through the door, he as Nunc Dimittis and she as Magnificat.

Ian and Sue McLeish

Bringer of Joy

My brother Duncan has a beautiful cat of various dark brown colours and her name is Chocolate. His surname is Button, so the vets absolutely love calling them into the surgery. I used to have an equally beautiful cat and his name was Jupiter, named after the Bringer of Joy. He gave us 18 years' worth of joy, too. He would often sleep on top of my wardrobe at night and leap onto my bed from a great height in the morning, so I never overslept! As a kitten, he would also sleep in a tissue box whenever he saw one, and when he was fully grown, he still used to sleep in them, although it was much harder for him to wriggle his elbows through the hole – but somehow he would manage it and would sit purring happily while 'making puddings' in the tissues with his claws, a blissful smile on his face. Another strange thing he used to do was to run and leap onto my back as I bent down to take clothes out of the washing basket, then cling on with his paws round my neck. He'd stay there all the time while I walked up and down hanging out the washing, occasionally hitching himself back up if he started to slip!

Linda Weeks

Cabbage cat

My cat Crackle used to bring us cabbage leaves as presents – not green ones, but really wet, soggy yellowy ones, twice her size! She would carry them in her mouth from the vegetable garden next door, often dragging them through the hedge hanging down on each side. On damp days, we would find these soggy leaves all over the house – up the stairs, under the table, even on the bed. She always seemed so proud of her find. One day her little face appeared at the window, almost completely obscured by an old birds' nest! She was a lovely little cat, whom I bottle-fed from two days old, as her mother abandoned her and she lived until the ripe old age of 18.

Jean Heath

Ahoy there!

We were having a family break in Hampshire visiting relatives one May. We were staying in a lovely bed and breakfast place and the hosts' cat had had kittens. My daughter Martha, then aged three, adored these kittens and was invited to cuddle them and we ended up travelling home to Norfolk with a little black and white kitten, hopping from lap to back seat to parcel shelf for the four- to five-hour journey. Once home, we quickly bought bed, bedding and tray, but our little feline friend rejected the bed and took to the 'Captain's' chair, refusing to sleep anywhere else. We call it the Captain's chair, as it is the kind of chair a captain used and twizzled round in whilst navigating. Hence the kitten was named Captain.

Paula and Martha Jones

I heard that, pardon?

In the late 1980s I had a lovely cat that really thought he was human. I named him Staveley, after a character in a TV series called *I Didn't Know You Cared*. He was an old deaf chap who carried the ashes of his commander in a box tied round his neck, and used to say, 'I heard that, pardon?' to everyone. His name was Uncle Staveley and I thought it was a great name for my new kitten. Also at that time, Dave Lee-Travis was a DJ on Radio 1 and I decided to give my beloved cat the middle name of Travis, so he became Staveley Travis. It produced some very strange looks in the vet's waiting room over the years.

Kathryn Newman

Confident cat

Our first cat was Sampson, whom we had for nearly 18 years. He was a great hunter and would catch almost fully grown rabbits, bringing them in at night under our bed and we would wake to hear crunching and slurping sounds as he ate his way through same. Our second cat, Strudle, was so gentle that if she caught a daddy long-legs, she thought she'd been on a big game hunt! Our next cat was Dexter, a rescue cat. We had him from the RSPCA, he was very frightened and timid and had been there for seven months. On bringing him home, he vanished and, after much searching, we found him on top of the kitchen units. He remained there for the next five weeks! He only came down at night to eat and use his tray. We brought in a short pair of steps and climbed up to talk to him and stroke him while he cowered against the wall. It was three weeks before we were rewarded with a purr! I talked to him even if I couldn't see him whenever I was in the kitchen. Finally, after five weeks, he started to come down, timidly and fearfully exploring his new home. Now, three years later, he is a lovable and loving puss of some 15 pounds (the vet suggests he lose a pound or two!) who goes to sleep on our laps, tummy upwards, with his tiny pink tongue poking out. It was definitely more than worthwhile persevering with this once-nervous cat, to help him regain his confidence.

Maureen M. Ledbury

Window cat

Our late lamented blue point, Wokki, had a voice like a banshee and the build and stamina of a Jack Russell terrier. He taught himself to open windows by scrabbling up the glass and pushing up the catch with his nose, then heaving himself through the top window. One evening, as my husband and I were preparing for an outing, Wokki began hiccuping violently. The babysitter arrived, but we decided to take the cat to see the vet first. On returning we put him on his feet, whereupon he promptly collapsed and lay prone on the kitchen floor. A quick call to the vet revealed that he had been given an injection of muscle relaxant and to put him somewhere quiet, as he would be unconscious until morning. So we took his bed into the bedroom upstairs, tenderly laying him down next to the radiator, locked him in and set off on our outing. On our return later that evening, the babysitter greeted us with 'That blooming cat!' Apparently, five minutes after we had gone, there had been an unholy racket at the back door. On opening it, she had been greeted by Wokki howling in protest. He swept past her with a withering look, went into the sitting room and settled in front of the fire for the evening.

Marilyn Midgley

Namesake

I used to work in Bath for a firm of solicitors, and my boss was a lovely man called Lance, now sadly long gone. I was living with my parents at the time and thought I could do with some company so, having heard of some kittens needing homes, I went off one lunchtime to have a look. One little black and white bundle won me over, needless to say, so I departed back to the office with him in a cardboard box. My colleague and I had our own office, so the little chap was soon out of his box and finding things to play with. It wasn't long before my boss came into our office and saw the little kitten. But he wasn't cross, far from it. He spent some time talking to the kitten and stroking it, and when he left our office I decided to call the kitten 'Lance', after my boss. I told my boss the next time he visited our office and he seemed flattered. My boss would often come to my parents' home on social visits and he was highly amused when I called out, 'Lance, come and have a cuddle,' or 'I don't know what I would do without you, Lance!'

Mikki Hayes

Stool pigeon

My two previous cats were called Jasper and Jason and were two little pickles, always up to mischief. One day I found a live pigeon sitting on a plant in the dining room. Another time I discovered a complete birds' nest in the kitchen. I imagined Jason pushing it through the cat flap and Jasper pulling it on the other side!

Jean Armstrong

Extraordinary cat

Living with my cat Snuggles was a lifelong adventure, full of unexpected surprises. As he was deaf, I reckon he was extra intelligent. He was trained to accept a harness, which did have its delights. I was able to take him for walks in the local high street and one of his many delights was to have me help him climb – me pushing him up by his hind legs – and sit on the post box outside the bakery and watch people and traffic go by. Many a person was startled by his white tail swishing in front of the pillar-box letter opening. When he got bored with this, he would jump down on to the traffic light control box, go to the pedestrian crossing, and we would proceed with dignity to cross the road. On one particular occasion a dog on a lead was coming towards us, and I'm sure the car drivers were expecting a 'dust-up'. However, the dog didn't seem to be able to believe his eyes and turned to look at Snuggles, nearly dislocating his neck. Snuggles, of course, did what any self-respecting cat would do and looked straight ahead with his head held high. He also had a favourite shop that he insisted on going in and he would inspect every inch of the shop before leaving. The staff were very understanding and looked forward to his visits. We were even televised once walking round the shops and the local children thought it was a great hoot! Snuggles was taught hand signals and responded very well to them. I was once asked why I spoke to Snuggles when he was deaf. I replied that he could lip read! Well, what else could I say?

Eileen Hunter

Clever thief

My brown Burmese cat arrived home one day carrying a whole hard-boiled egg (uncracked). However, his best achievement by far was to arrive home proudly carrying an unopened tin of sardines. Not only is my cat a thief . . . but he can also read!

Shirley Jones

Changing names

As a family, we are pretty hopeless at choosing names for our cats because we tend to shorten, lengthen, or change them! For instance, Mitzi became Mittles; Twinkles became Twinks (a fairly normal abbreviation by our standards!), then Twizzle to Twig to Twizzy-Wizz! And then there was Ee-Wee, who started out as Thingy, because we were not supposed to be keeping her – the theory being that if we didn't name her, the parting would be easier. Our vet refused to write Thingy on her vaccination certificate, so he wrote Lucky instead, but by this time she had become Ingy Thingy or Ingles! Four years later, our daughter was born and her first attempt at saying the name came out as Ee-Wee. She was an extraordinary cat. She once carried a moorhen over a seven-foot fence, in through the bedroom fanlight window and deposited it under our bed (difficult, as moorhens have very large feet!). She lived to nearly 20 and was much loved.

Judith Doyle

Double trouble

My cat Tabouleh, born in the Middle East, performed some strange antics in his time. Once, after being 'banged up' in quarantine for six months, he came home to a new bungalow and, being a typical cat, was very inquisitive. One very cold morning, I decided to cook a beef casserole and, upon taking the casserole dish out to stir the contents, was mortified to see two huge amber eyes peering at me through the vents above the oven. I panicked, wondering how Tabouleh had got into the oven housing above the built-in cooker, deliberating whether or not I should ring the fire brigade to get him released. I found the kitchen steps and reached up over the cooker housing to find that the builder had failed to fit a mesh cover, hence Tabouleh was able to climb down into the cooker area, having jumped onto the working area and onto the cooker hob, and then up and down into the housing unit. The smell of the casserole cooking and the warmth of the cooker had evidently enticed him up there. Needless to say, he eventually came down of his own accord.

Sadly, Tabouleh is no longer with us, but he had a very active life, was in quarantine three times and was always in trouble.

Mrs B. McDermott

Flowers for the lady

My lilac Siamese cat is called Ty Lou and absolutely loves carnations. He finds them irresistible and will pick them out of a vase of flowers and deposit them at my bedroom door, or at my feet. Recently my neighbour called to tell me that when she opened her back door that morning she had a bouquet of carnations on her step, neatly spread out.

Sheila Alexander

Cat burglar

Socks came to live with us when he was three months old, a little ball of black and white fur with white socks on his front paws and white boots on his back paws, hence the name. When he was six months old and allowed out, his outings gradually took him further away from our garden and our neighbours' gardens. He began to bring things home, starting with pieces of silver paper and cellophane from cigarette packets, pieces of string, plastic strips, old drinking straws, cardboard cups, old bits of car components and dynamo brushes. From these meagre beginnings, he graduated to all sizes and shapes of socks, ladies' gloves and children's mittens. One day he came walking down the path dragging a tea towel behind him. Another day, he brought us a small Action Man, plus an arm and leg from another one! Of course, we also had the more usual frogs, birds and feathers brought home too.

About six months ago we came home to find clumps of mud in the lounge and kitchen. As I was cleaning up the mud, my husband Tom pointed out something shiny, which we washed in the kitchen sink. It was a broken gold bracelet and to this day we have no idea where he found it. I had the bracelet repaired and it's lovely. Socks, now seven and very handsome, still brings us presents. We have adopted a sister for him, called Tosca. She was found in Ascot Woods when she was only six weeks old and her name is Ascot spelt backwards, with some transposition of the 's' and 'c'. She gives Socks a hard time, but they love each other really.

Eve Lomax

Fatalistic tale

This is a rather sad tale for a cat's name. Years ago when my boss had a new cat, he was asked what he had called it. 'Next,' he replied. When asked why, he answered that it was 'Because it will be the next one to get run over.'

Ann Wolfe

Fearless felines

Many years ago, when four of our six cats were kittens, about four weeks old, their mother was killed by a post office van. Pops, a black and white male (not their father), took over their welfare. On this particular day, he had carried all four kittens to the front of the house and was affectionately guarding them, when a large Alsatian and Labrador dog arrived. They immediately ran at Pops from opposite sides. Pops crouched down motionless. Just as both dogs were about to bite, Pops did a 'Bruce Lee' vertical leap and the two dogs collided. But Pops was not finished. He turned in mid-air and landed on the back of the surprised Alsatian and proceeded to claw his nostrils and bite into his neck. With a ghastly yelp, the dog hared off down the drive with Pops on his back. Leaping off after a few yards, Pops returned post-haste and immediately set upon the

Labrador, who didn't wait and followed the already disappearing Alsatian. I viewed this all helplessly from an upstairs window.

Ninja, our female 10-year-old, is no less courageous. She loves going out in the rain and we have a deep pond that never seems to deter her – she waits on the bank and dives on unsuspecting moorhens and swims back after her diving efforts. She climbs electricity poles past the barbed wire. She once brought home a pheasant twice her size! But her most amazing exploit is her ability to catch and play with full-grown adders. She catches them at the back of the hedge and brings them into the garage. She then plays so that she is just out of striking distance. The snake keeps striking until it over-stretches and Ninja then darts in and catches the snake at the back of the head. This continues until the exhausted reptile has no more 'go' left. I usually let the snake rest and then take him a few fields away to continue his life unmolested.

Trefor N. Hughes

Irish connections

My husband and I had been married for quite some time and were longing to start a family, but it just seemed like it was not to be, so we got a cat instead. We were going to have a little black kitten, but when we went to pick her up there was just one other kitten left – a white and barred tiger – so we took her as well. I had already decided to call mine Leilah, which means black as night, and my husband decided to call the other one Tara, after his favourite TV character Tara King in *The Avengers*. About eight years later I discovered I was pregnant. We were delighted when our beautiful daughter was born. She has stunning titian hair and that, together with the fact that I am of Irish descent, made Tara seem the most appropriate name. The grandparents were horrified that we seemed to be naming our child after the cat, but we wouldn't have used the name for the cat had we known we were going to be blessed with our daughter. It was all happily resolved when Tara began to talk and said, 'Mi Ya Ya,' meaning 'my Tara' – so puss became known as Miyaya. Her twin Leilah had only kept her name for about a week, as she had an absolute fascination for feet and especially toes, so she became Toots. So Leilah and Tara became Toots and Miyaya!

Pat Poole

Paddling cat

When my daughter Jessica was three, we got a little black and white kitten called Rosie. I was actually on my way to the supermarket, passed the pet shop, fell in love with this adorable bundle of fluff and blew the housekeeping money on a kitten! Rosie turned into an amazingly human cat. She would give kisses on request and loved nothing more than having a bath. She would always sit on the side of the bath when either I or Jess were in it, and would invariably jump in for a paddle when the water was draining away. We were both highly amused by her antics and one day, Jess was in the bathroom when Rosie jumped in for a paddle. Jess came marching up to me, hands on hips, and announced, 'Mummy, Rosie's got no sympathy – she's in the bath again!' I'm still not sure what she meant, but it was very funny!

Michaela O'Neill

Completely crackers!

Ever since I moved into my own home when I was 21, I have always had two cats. Although there are many funny tales to tell, by far the most amusing one is about a cat called Jacob – not named, as my grandmother had hoped, after a religious character, but after the cream crackers, because he was beige and cream. At the time, I had a cylinder vacuum cleaner which I dragged around the house. Every so often, I would drag it a bit too vigorously and it would roll over and depress the on/off switch, turning it off. So when the cleaner suddenly began to switch off every two or three minutes, I immediately thought that

I had caused the problem by being too physical with the thing. But each time I went to the cleaner, it was the right way up. There didn't seem to be a logical explanation. Secreting myself behind the door post, I switched the rather noisy cleaner on, then observed in amazement as Jacob ran full pelt at the cleaner, jumped up in the air and landed with all his weight and both front paws directly on the button! After that, I had to vacuum with a plastic cup taped over the button.

Jayne Jones

Haughty and naughty

We are fortunate to have living with us two Burmans: Araminta, a haughty four-year-old female who came from the Blue Cross, and George, a three-year-old naughty boy, son of a supreme champion, over a stone of mischief and trouble. George's favourite eats include oranges, peaches, mango, banana, apple, rice pudding, yoghurt, Liquorice Allsorts, bacon sandwiches and anything else my husband will share with him. He will go to our neighbours' house in the afternoons when we are both at work, get on the chair next to Reg (now 88) then go to sleep and keep Reg awake with his noisy snoring! He has developed the skill of opening packages containing cat treats, cupboard doors and anything else that may have had food stored in it at some time. He sleeps on his back stretched out across the settee, almost covering both seats, and is most put out if you wish to sit there too. Araminta, in contrast, is the perfect lady who will visit you only when she sees fit and is in need of a little fuss. Together they give us hours of fun and entertainment.

Elizabeth Elliott-Smith

Scottish cats

In 1995 work took us to the Moray Coast in Scotland and whilst there we rented a farmhouse nestling in the hills between the town of Forres and Elgin. We decided that, living on a farm, we should have cats, so just before the move we visited a litter to take two kittens north of the border. As it happened, there were only three males left and my wife Margaret immediately announced that we would take all three, as she didn't want to choose and leave one on its own. We spent the time on the 10-hour journey north choosing names for the three kittens. One was easy – he became Felix, as he was the spitting image of the cat on the can. However, we wanted the other two to have Scottish names, although one was black with half a white face and we were very tempted to call him Phantom (as in *Phantom of the Opera*). The other kitten, obviously the runt, was very small and totally black and had taken a shine to me, so was now 'my cat'. As my sport is motor rallying and that year Scotland's Colin McRae had just become World Rally Champion, my little black cat was named McRae, or Mac for short. That left 'half face'. We had visited the Moray Coast before the move and fallen in love with the tiny hamlet of Brodie with its lovely castle, so Brodie he became. So we had Felix, McRae and Brodie, but that was not the end of it. Some time after moving, we were fortunate enough to be invited to a social function at Brodie Castle and met the laird, a very distinguished and elegant gentleman resplendent in his clan tartan. He was known as Brodie of Brodie, so our cat with the fine Scottish name of Brodie is now called Bob for short!

Phil Terry

Fancy a joint?

I once had two adorable cats, brother and sister, from an RSPCA home. They loved me to pieces. Locked doors were no barrier to them seeking me out. The large orange tom used to batter doors down in order to reach his love. Wailing outside bedroom windows, scaling great heights, digging up carpets – these were nothing when trying to reach 'the hand that opens' in the morning. One Sunday morning, I slowly came to and wondered why the pesky pair had failed to break through the closed bedroom door, which they usually tunnelled under to creep into my bed. I trotted downstairs, called them, to no avail, saw that the kitchen door was open and let my mind fill with horrifying thoughts of catnappers. There was only silence. The earth must have stopped revolving, surely, for the cats not to have dragged me to the tin-opener hours earlier. But no; there they sat, side by side on the sofa, legs crossed, seemingly uninterested in the love of their life. Not a whisker twitched. Puzzled, I strode into the kitchen, flicked on the kettle and flung open the back door to take in the morning air. There, on the step, sat the largest joint of pork I have ever seen in my life. It was raw and had attracted a few flies. I instantly knew what had happened, so unusual had their guilty behaviour been. I still like to imagine the dastardly duo heaving their prize over the obligatory six-foot fence, only to be defeated by a cat flap too small to allow them to deliver their gift of love to their mummy. I disposed of the joint in the bin. I can only explain this ungrateful act as one that protected the criminals from discovery by hiding the evidence of the crime as quickly as possible. They couldn't have eaten it raw anyway!

Louise Smith

Best mates

Recently I was vacuuming the carpet in the dining room and the back door was open. As I vacuumed under the table, there was a very loud 'Miaow!' My wife Beverley shouted, 'Stop!

You've got its tail!' There was a loud miaowing and wailing and obviously a terrified cat was somewhere close by. Suddenly Ben, the black Labrador, jumped from his bed and rushed out of the back door with us in hot pursuit. We were just in time to see a huge grey cat holding our poor little Smokey down on his back. However, he was no match for Ben, who woofed and chased. The grey cat took off and tried to scale a 12-foot vertical wall. Realising that he was not Sherpa Tensing, he landed back at the feet of a very excited Ben, picked himself up and took off down the garden. He was chased at great speed by a great, bounding and very happy Ben. Luckily for the grey cat, he got over the fence and away. The dog, tongue hanging out like Dick Dastardly's Muttley, trotted back to Smokey and started licking him all over. Smokey purred and walked all around the dog, rubbing himself against Ben. They then went into the basket and lay down, the cat snuggled in tight against the dog!

John Sheen

Foiled again!

Boo, my brown Burmese, was in the kitchen guarding the joint of lamb that was resting under the tin foil. When the phone rang, my husband answered it but, being worried about leaving Boo and joint in the same room, quickly hurried back to the kitchen to check on the joint. Looking at the table, the foil was still on the joint and all looked well, so he went back to the call. When he'd finished the call, he returned to the kitchen and still all looked fine, but he could hear a strange noise. On investigating the noise coming from under the kitchen table, he found Boo and a half-eaten joint of lamb. He checked the foil and obviously the joint was gone, but the foil was still in the shape of the joint. The cheeky little monster had slipped his paw under the foil and swiped the joint off the board, but had left the foil in the same position!

Liz Holmes

Saved by the cat

I bought my cat, Lucybelle Sheena Domino LaCat, from a pet shop some nine years ago. I wanted a gentle little cat for my birthday present and there were lots of pretty kittens in the shop but, no – Lucy chose me. I got her home and introduced her to my lovely collie dog, when my gentle cat decided it would be fun to beat the hell out of me! For ages, as she was growing up, I was covered in scratches, pouring blood from my chest where she climbed up me in my nightie, and slid down again with claws out. Friends suggested that we should part company, but I decided she should stay or someone else would have her put down.

One day she literally saved my life. I was cooking some plums on the hob one evening about 8 p.m., thinking I could have them later with some custard, but then I was distracted by something and had gone to bed around 10.30 p.m. Lucy came in and decided to start scratching the bed, something she doesn't normally do. I got up and went to the loo, only to catch sight of the plums in the glass pan about to explode! It was then 4.30 a.m.!

Lindsay M. Turner

You've been licked!

We have a new kitten called Muffin. I had just passed some GCSEs and was going out to dinner with some friends to celebrate. I wasn't going to have any tea because we would be eating at 8 o'clock, but as I was particularly hungry, I thought I'd pick at any leftovers. The children had had sausage casserole and mashed potatoes for tea, and I looked on with delight as I saw a tray sporting a plate with a sausage and some mash left over. I carefully sliced up the sausage, popped it into a bowl with the potato and poured on some hot gravy to warm it up. Then I sat on the sofa tucking in hungrily. 'Muffin likes sausages and mashed potato,' piped up Natalie. 'Does she?' I replied distractedly – I was really enjoying my leftovers. 'Yes, she licked both and really enjoyed it,' replied Natalie. 'Did you give her some?' I asked. 'No,' said Natalie, 'she had what Alexandra left on her tray.' It was then, looking at Muffin, paws akimbo, cleaning her bits and bobs, that I realised that the very tasty sausage and mash I was so enjoying had been 'Muffined'!

Kim Howe

Mousey surprise

When my cat Molly was a year old she discovered the joys of mousing. I had brought a holdall home from work, full of paperwork that I intended to do at home, but it remained at the bottom of the stairs all night untouched. Before leaving for work the next day, I saw Molly jumping in and out of the holdall, as was her wont. The holdall remained under my desk all day at work – I was still too busy to look at the backlog – and I duly brought it home again that night. On dropping the bag at the bottom of the stairs, the waiting Molly immediately jumped in and out, triumphantly holding a dead mouse in her mouth. I had sat all day at work with a dead mouse in my bag!

Ruth Scott

Hidden pong?

About ten years ago we had a cat called Scrauper, a lovely black and white female. The name Scrauper, according to my father-in-law, meant messing about. We came home from work one evening to find a horrible pong in the lounge. My wife and I tried to track it down to no avail; drains, vases of flowers and everything else was checked. After about an hour, I pulled the sofa away from the wall to find a whole piece of plaice, complete with breadcrumbs, which looked rather bedraggled from having been pulled through the cat flap. We never did find out where it came from, but we have a good laugh about it even now.

Anthony Morgan

Jess the cat

We go to a farm once a week to see the farmer's wife who is 89 and almost bedridden, to help with anything she needs doing. Like all farms, this one has cats and they did run wild but, as my wife saves them scraps which she brings every week, they have got used to us. We were tempted to have one of the kittens but we didn't succumb until about a year ago, because we get very heavy traffic where we live and, having lost a cat to traffic previously, we'd said we wouldn't have another. So we took home a little tabby kitten that had been abandoned by its mother. It was only half the size of its siblings and had one rear leg out of its socket, but it showed such spirit and determination that we decided to give it a chance, road or not. My wife decided that because it was so small and looked pregnant, it was a female and we would stand a good chance if we kept her in at night. We took her straight to the vet, who said her temperature was way over normal, her stomach was swollen with worms (not pregnant) and she was less than half normal weight. He said he would try and reset the leg before operating, but not to build up our hopes because she was extremely poorly.

After a month in plaster, Jessica, as my wife had named her, made a good recovery. We kept her in until we thought she was at least six months, then took her to the vet to be spayed – whereupon he pronounced her to be a tom! This was despite her having been examined and operated upon by three different vets earlier. He is now Jess, which fortunately is a unisex name, so the transition was quite easy.

Terry Free

Hidden gift

We have two cats, Titten, a black cat who was never really named properly and Buzz, who is grey and tabby. After moving house a year ago, we were lucky enough to find ourselves next door to a brilliant couple, who are also very good cat sitters. Earlier this year, we treated ourselves to a long weekend in Italy and the cat sitting was arranged for morning and evening, so we didn't have to worry about the cats. The day following our return, we were thanking the neighbours over the fence and telling them about our trip when I noticed Titten popping under the fence into the neighbours' garden. She disappeared for a moment, then reappeared into view behind the couple we were conversing with. My partner was just handing over a lovely bottle of wine and saying 'Cheers' when Titten jumped into a large half-barrel planter, dug a small shallow hole and said thank you in her own small way. I just kept smiling and talking gibberish until the evidence was covered and the cat had disappeared back into the shrubbery. No harm done… until replanting time, that is!

Honor Auld

Cat on the dole

My brother Steve owned a cat when he lived in Manchester some years ago. At the time, Steve was unemployed and was given a kitten whom he called Giro, because he said it only got fed properly once a fortnight when he got his unemployment benefit!

Andy Burton

Six lives left

My very dark tiger stripe tabby Humphrey managed to lose three lives in the space of three weeks last year. You get a great deal of cat for your money where Humphrey is concerned – he weighs in at 14 pounds of solid cat (he is not fat). I suddenly noticed that he seemed exceptionally thin and the wrong shape so, with some difficulty, I carted him off to the vet. After examining him, the vet said that he must have received a massive blow to his mid-section because all his organs were pushed up into his chest and there were none left in the middle. This, of course, entailed a very expensive operation and the vet instructed that Humphrey should stay indoors for a week. I put him in the spare bedroom because it only has a small fanlight right at the top of the window. I had only been at work about half an hour when I had a frantic call from my father to say that Humphrey had just walked in through the cat flap and I must have left the bedroom door open. I raced home, checked the bedroom door, but it was closed. This meant that he could only have got out through the fanlight and jumped down at least eight feet onto the garden table in the courtyard.

I retrieved Humphrey and put him in the front bedroom which has a higher fanlight, so I was sure he could not tackle it. Again, there was another frantic call from Father – Humphrey had just walked in through the cat flap again. Again I checked the bedroom door – closed! This time he must have clawed his way to the top of the window, somehow got through a very limited space, possibly onto the window sill, and then jumped down approximately 12-15 feet into the front garden. And all this the day after an operation with his stitches still in place. After a rather strained phone call to the vet, he advised that it was useless trying to keep Humphrey indoors, as he was doing more damage than if he was just left to his own devices. He made a swift and perfectly ordinary recovery and was back to his old 14-pound self very quickly. It's just as well they have nine lives!

Anne from Southampton

Champion fisherman

About 15 years ago I had a lovely cat called Smokey, who was a darling, but he had a passion for fishing that would make John Wilson look like a part-timer. Smokey would arrive home with live fan-tailed goldfish and live koi carp that were by no means small. They would be presented to me on the rug in the living room. The fish would then be transferred to the waiting bucket and given to a friend who had a pond, after having tried to find out who they belonged to, with no luck. My friend David was very grateful and said that some of the fish that Smokey brought home were very expensive to buy. Smokey brought around 20 fish home, all in fully working order, and some of them are still swimming around in David's pond today!

Raymond Hewlett

A cautionary tale

Like all cat owners, when one of my two cats, Smartie or Fergus, goes missing for some unusual length of time I start to worry, even though I know cats change their habits regularly and nine times out of ten they come strolling in with a 'What's all the fuss for?' air about them. But on this occasion, Smartie wasn't home for his tea, wasn't home for his night-time cuddle and wasn't home for breakfast. By lunchtime I had asked all the neighbours, but nobody had seen him. Late in the afternoon I left tearful, worried children and went out searching the country lanes and calling his name. I began to fear the worst. Suddenly, I heard the sound of running footsteps, and my son Oliver came running round the corner shouting, 'He's back! He's back!' then, rather bemusingly, 'The carpet man has brought him back!'

The day before, a man had come to lay a carpet in the house. Smartie must have thought the van, with its tantalising open door, looked an interesting place to explore. He must have been rather surprised when the door was slammed shut and the van trundled off to the carpet fitter's home, some 20 miles away. Smartie stayed trapped until the middle of the next day, when the man, hearing strange sounds, discovered that he had more than just carpets in his van. Luckily, he had the sense not to let the cat escape and by powers of deduction, worked out that he must belong to us. Smartie was none the worse for his adventure, just pleased to be home, if a little grumpy at having missed several meals. The children, however, noticed a rather unpleasant smell coming from inside the van, so it would seem that Smartie had exacted his revenge in the way only a tom-cat can!

Lynnsay Dulley

Shake a leg!

I was living in a fraternity house in New Brunswick in the USA in the early 90s, sleeping on the floor in a room full of rubbish. I was regularly woken up by a cat called Djibouti (as in the state in north-east Africa) who belonged to the fraternity house. The cat would climb in through the window at about 5 a.m. and go round waking everybody up by snuggling up to their faces! Djibouti would thus make a nuisance of himself until somebody got up to feed him, whereupon he would disappear for the rest of the day, only to resume the next morning. The cat was really sweet and everyone talked about Djibouti in reverential tones.

Jacek Koba

Fond memories

Pebbles was a rescue cat from the RSPCA, about five years old. She was mostly black, although her chest, chin, one ear and one leg were all white. She had a black splodge on her nose that gave her a constant frowning look. She was very much a 'lap cat' and loved attention. This was partly because her previous owner had mistreated her – she had been beaten after having kittens and suffered several broken ribs and missing teeth before she arrived at the RSPCA. As cats go, she was very intelligent and devious with it.

Our local paper is broadsheet-sized, and I used to spread it on the floor to read it. Pebbles always knew exactly which story I was reading, and would come and sit exactly on the spot to get my attention. If I was reclining in bed with Pebbles lying on my chest, and there was any hint of me dozing off, a little paw would stretch out and wrap itself around my nose, just in case I forgot to keep stroking. However, it was in the pursuit of food that Pebbles really excelled. Milk bottle tops were a delicacy. She learned to recognise the sound of the cupboard where the coffee was kept; coffee meant milk, and milk meant cream on the bottle cap! On opening the cupboard there would be a thud from upstairs and a small black missile would hurtle down the stairs to the kitchen to see if there was a bottle top going. She liked crisps and would happily beg for a Quaver or a Wotsit. If I wasn't careful, one might even be snatched on the way from the packet to my mouth.

TV dinners posed more of a problem. Pebbles would sit on the arm of the settee and study the contents of my plate. If I wasn't paying proper attention to my meal, I sometimes noticed a sneaky paw stretching out ever so slowly, trying to reach some tasty titbit. And batting the spaghetti dangling from my fork was also good sport.

And then there was the incident with the chip. Our dining table had a spare chair adjacent to mine, and Pebbles was allowed to sit on this at mealtimes, but not on my lap. One day, while we were eating, Pebbles decided that she wanted a lap. She climbed onto the spare chair, and continued onto my lap where she settled. I pushed her off onto the floor. A few minutes later, she tried again and was pushed onto the floor again. She made a third attempt and was back on the floor. It still amazes me what happened next. On the fourth attempt, she got onto the spare chair and went straight across my lap at speed, pausing only to grab a large chip from my plate before she jumped down and ran into the kitchen! Another time she was caught nibbling a chicken leg on the kitchen floor. This she had 'rescued' from the kitchen bin, having managed to open it using the pedal!

We have many other delightful memories of our little black and white friend: the way I could drape her round my neck like a fur stole; the way I could cuddle her in bed like a teddy bear; the way she dribbled on your lap through the gaps left by her missing teeth; and the way she could stay in her cat basket at the vet's, even if you tipped it on end and shook it!

Peter Jewell

A fishy tale

I have two cats called Felix and Toffee. One morning I was ready to leave for work when I spotted Felix playing with something in the garden. Rushing out I discovered to my horror that it was a goldfish; not just any old goldfish, but a large one with frilly fins and a big feathery tail. Luckily, Felix had just dropped it, so I managed to scoop it up in my hands and rush it indoors where I put it into a bucket of water. I had to leave for work, so I covered the bucket with clingfilm (with holes cut in it). I expected the fish to have died of shock during the course of the day, but when I got home that evening, it was happily swimming around, minus a few scales. None of our immediate neighbours have fishponds, so when my husband came home, he drove the car whilst I looked after the bucket and fish. We drove around the neighbourhood asking people if they had lost a fish, but without any luck. Finally, we left the fish with a lady who had a pond and offered to give it a home.

Jenny Dal Bello

Love thy neighbour

Cooper was a cream Burmese addicted to purloining the odd thing or two. My daughter spied him dragging something past the patio doors towards the kitchen door and cat flap. Alert, I rushed to the back door and, upon opening it, found a still steaming joint of meat on the step and a very pleased looking cat. Almost simultaneously came a knock at the front door. My husband answered it, to be confronted by our neighbour almost jumping up and down in anger. She explained what had happened, accused us of not feeding our cat and asked what we were going to do about it. I paid for the leg of lamb and made sure that Cooper had it chopped up on his dish for a week!

Judi Morgan

Cat combustion

One morning recently, as I was getting dressed, our youngest daughter Maria came running upstairs into our bedroom. She said,

'Dad, when you go down into the living room, you'll smell a strong whiff of singeing. Mum thought it was her hairdryer needing a clean out, but don't worry – it was only the cat! He doesn't look too bad and I've managed to remove most of the big, black scorch marks.' I immediately had visions of a half-roasted, half-furless animal prowling around. Maria then told me that Pepper had been lying in front of the gas fire and when he had got up and stretched his front paws, he had projected his tail and backside in the direction of the gas fire, with obvious consequences.

Derek Jago

No frontiers

I had a rescue cat called Barnaby when I first left home. He believed he was a dog and, other than barking, exhibited all the usual dog characteristics. He would fetch – if you threw a piece of string, he would retrieve it and drop it at your feet to play again. If he saw us walking to the station in the morning, he would follow us; he came on a walking holiday to the Lakes with us, sporting a bright red harness, and tramped about the fields.

However, the most embarrassing thing of all was Barnaby's lack of understanding of boundaries. He regarded all cat flaps as doors for him. If we went out, he went in next door's (or anyone else's) cat flap, ate their cat's food and slept on their cat's bed. He became very well known where we lived on a new estate, especially when he found the nearby show house was always open, warm in winter with visitors passing through to pet him, as they came across a real, live, grubby cat sleeping on the white bed linen on their mini beds! The most embarrassing occasion, however, was when he went to see the neighbours one day, ate their unsupervised semi-frozen lamb chops defrosting in the kitchen and, discovering that he was rather full, went to lie down on their bed for a few hours. They brought back a slumbering heap of cat with a very fat stomach, luckily seeing the funny side of it.

We are still waiting to hear which neighbour lost their goldfish – all we found were a few scales on our kitchen floor and a cat with wet paws!

Jeremy Page

Noble name

Many years ago we decided to call our moggie Cuthbert – a noble name for a great cat. Cuthbert is one of the few cats I know of who is named after a bishop (Cuthbert Bardsley, Bishop of Coventry at the time), who was also on the board of a major football club (Coventry City F. C.). One evening (back in the 60s and at the time of Christiaan Barnard), we were carrying out a mock heart transplant on Cuthbert, only to find that we were not entirely correct in our gender specification – yes, Cuthbert was a 'she'.

John T. Downey

Bike or cat?

When my husband John was five years old, he wanted a bike for his birthday like all his friends had, but because they lived on a hill, he was given a cat instead. John called the cat Raleigh!

Helen Harris

After you!

I took my grandchildren home from school one day a few years ago, and they went into the kitchen and called out, 'Grandma, there's a bird in here.' Thinking there was a body to dispose of, I was amazed to see a magpie sitting on the cats' food bowl with the two cats, Theo and Herne, just looking on. We quickly put the cats into another room, then opened the patio door and out hopped the magpie. I am still puzzled as to how he got through the cat flap. Did Theo and Herne hold it open for him, I wonder?

Barbara Ferrier

Strange tastes

We named our cat Ding-Dong because we were in the middle of having a 'ding-dong' when the person from the Cats Protection League brought him to us, and we had to stop when the door-bell went 'ding-dong', hence the name. He is large and grey, doesn't like fish very much, but loves raw blackcurrants and raw sprouts!

Dorothy Brilton

Mum and Dad's namesakes

We have two tabby cats who are brother and sister, about nine months old. They are called Tilly and Alfie, after my mother and father, Matilda and Alfred, now sadly long gone. I often wonder what they would have thought of having cats named after them. Tilly thinks she's a dog – she has a plastic ball with a bell in it and she loves to run after it and bring it back when you throw it. Alfie is content with playing with an antistatic brush, which he runs around with in his mouth.

Alan Kendrick

Postman cat!

We got George, our beautiful black and white cat, from the local cat rescue home and he had only been with us a short while when we had my six-year-old nephew, Andrew, to stay. Early on the Sunday morning, there was a lot of commotion, which roused Andrew, and he got up to investigate. He shouted outside my parents' bedroom door: 'Grandma, there's a cat's paw coming through the letterbox!' My Mum, believing it was the usual early morning Sunday paper delivery, said, 'No, it's just the paper, Andrew. Go back to bed,' in the hope that she could get a few more minutes' lie-in. However, the noise persisted and we were amazed and amused to discover that not only had George discovered the front door, but he was also trying – successfully – to rouse somebody to let him in by rattling the letterbox! From then on, whenever he wanted to be let in, he would rattle the letterbox with his paw poking through.

Another of our cats, Maisy, was very fond of hunting and bringing her trophies back to the kitchen for us. On two such occasions, we were honoured with treasures other than the usual mouse or shrew. One afternoon I was busy ironing when Maisy dashed in with something in her mouth. On looking closer I could see that it wasn't her usual catch. I stooped down to try to get her to release whatever she had caught, and to my shock she carefully placed on the carpet an entirely whole and very much alive bumble bee about the size of a 50 pence coin. Amazingly, she hadn't been stung. On another occasion, while Mum and I were watching TV, we were disturbed by a great wailing at the back door. Positive that Maisy must be hurt in some way, we jumped up with alarm and rushed to the back door to let her in. Maisy rushed past us into the kitchen and hid under the table. We peered down and were astonished to see her with a whole bird's nest in her mouth. She was particularly proud of this find and wouldn't let us anywhere near her, and proceeded to run around the house with us in hot pursuit, leaving feathers, straw and bits of nest all over the place. Sad to say we no longer have any cats, but these two brought us a lot of love and laughter in their short lives.

Diane Lund

Burns' cats

I currently have a semi-furry black and white tom-cat with a bushy tail and a generally grumpy attitude called Haggis. My husband suggested Haggis for a joke and the name stuck. From behind when he's walking along with his tail in the air, he looks like a skunk. My friend Ann thinks he looks more like Batman with his black head and white nose and mouth. At times when he is really grumpy, he looks like an old-fashioned robber and should have a bag of swag slung over his shoulder. This is not inappropriate, as he once got locked in a neighbour's house and proceeded to eat their chicken pieces, which were defrosting on the worktop. He has also been seen being dismissed from another kitchen by a lady who was obviously baking on a summer's day with the back door open. And to think I was prepared to get another two and call them Neeps and Tatties!

Sarah A. C. Bailey

Strange new toy

Once I was house and cat sitting for my sister. I was watching television one evening when I heard the cat, Roger, scrabbling around behind the sofa. After a while, I could ignore him no more and went to see what he was scratching at. I was faced with a large, pink belly, which I picked up to discover it belonged to a hamster! Though rather old and disturbingly lumpy, it was very calm and sat in my hand while Roger jumped at my legs for his new 'toy' back. I took the hamster on a tour of the neighbours to find out where he had come from, to no avail. Finally, at one house a mother let her two children take him in to live with their gerbils. I told my sister the whole story when she came back, but we never did find out where the hamster came from.

Amanda J. Wright

Ginger mauler

Some years ago my daughter bought two cats and two dogs from a rescue centre. The cats she called Caitlin and Megan and the dogs Helen and Troy. As they were all very young, they got on well. One day, Megan was out and about in the surrounding houses and fields and Troy was in the back yard. Megan was on her way home when she was set upon by the local 'ginger mauler'. Fleeing in terror, while screeching and yowling in fear, she fled down the alleyway between the houses to seek the shelter of home just over the back gate. Troy, hearing her cries and obviously concerned, came to the back gate and stood some five feet back, awaiting her arrival. Megan came over the gate and shot between Troy's legs and into the house. The 'ginger mauler' came flying over the gate in hot pursuit to be greeted by the sight of T. Dog, as he is affectionately known, crouching back ready to pounce with teeth bared. To this day we have no idea how this cat did it, but he turned in mid-air and scrabbled his way back up over the gate with Troy snapping at his tail. He never bothered Megan again.

Bruce Parkin

Strange gifts

We have always had eccentric cats (something to do with the owners, apparently) but Luba, our ginger and white female, brought back some very odd things. A favourite trick of hers was to bring in large earthworms, which she buried in the sock bucket with the dirty socks (most unpleasant on wash day!). Later, these were supplemented by 50 pence pieces. We never found out where she got them from, but they went in the sock bucket too. Another cat, Toby, was not a hunter, despite his enormous size, but one day he caught a swift and brought it gently to us in his mouth. We released it and it flew away. As swifts never land, we have no idea how he got it, but he was very proud of it.

Carolyn Clarke

Flying Burman

When he was a kitten, Nye, our blue Burman decided to check out life outside and climbed out of a window on the first floor, which was only open a couple of notches for ventilation. Somehow, he ascended onto the concrete path below and was shaken, but otherwise unharmed. Burmans will always find a way out or a way in to wherever you do not want them to be; that is the nature of the beast. They are, after all, sacred and can do just as they please!

Elinor Bostock

Drink problem

My cat, Fudge, is 18 and is getting increasingly eccentric, mainly by insisting on drinking out of the loo, preferably freshly flushed! As a result, she follows anyone to the loo and just waits expectantly until they have finished. When my friend came to visit recently, she was taken aback, to put it mildly. When visiting the bathroom in the night, she found Fudge upside down in the loo!

Pat Dodd

A one-off

My cat is called Scrakey Bake and this name was chosen to describe the piercing cry she emits when she wants attention ('bake' in Ulster means face or mouth). I'm sure this must be a one-off name.

Maureen Doonan

Mouser with a difference

My cat Bill was a brilliant mouse catcher, but he never killed them. This was a problem as he would bring them in through the cat flap and let them go. One day in particular, he came in early with a mouse, dropped it and watched it run away, with me screaming for my husband to get up. Having chased the mouse all round the kitchen, the mouse decided to take refuge under the cat, and we had to pick Bill up and out ran the mouse. Evidently, he must have thought that Bill was his friend and felt safe with him. The mouse promptly disappeared under the washing machine and it took us about a month to catch it, as it would come out at night and feed out of the cat's bowl – I saw this happen often! When we pulled the washing machine out, we could not see it, until one day we noticed pieces of torn carpet and the mouse had made a nest up inside the machine.

Bill was also brilliant at catching a pencil. If you threw it he would bring it back to you like a dog would. He also used to steal small, sparkly objects such as earrings and he would hide them in different places in the house, like a magpie.

Beryl Clarke

Food games

I have a year-old ginger cat, which I was given nearly a year ago, when it was six weeks old. It had lived in stables with horses and wasn't used to humans. I christened it Joe and the following day took it to my friendly vet, who treated it for worms and fleas. We had to rename her – I was assured she was a Josephine, which is quite rare in all-ginger cats. She was initially very nervous and viewed me with great suspicion. I was advised by the vet to feed her on a diet of biscuits only, and not to let her drink milk. I went home with Josephine and a huge bag of biscuits. However, she turned up her nose at them and refused a nice saucer of water. The following day, she still wouldn't eat the prescribed dry food and hadn't had a drink. I rang the surgery and was told to be strong, not to give in, and she would eventually eat. I must admit the biscuits looked dull and I picked one up to have a closer look. It was very small and I dropped it. Josephine pounced on it, patted it a little, and then ate it! So I tossed another one at her. She chased it, killed it and ate that one too. Mealtimes after that became rather long, drawn-out affairs, but never boring. This pantomime went on for a few weeks and the habit was broken only when she had to spend a short time in a cattery. I imagine the busy staff didn't have the time to play cat and mouse with her!

Mary Good

It's that BC again!

A couple of years ago I bought a nice new washer-dryer. After only a few weeks I had problems. It wouldn't empty, so I called an engineer who couldn't give me an appointment for a week. I was quite cross – a new machine and having to wait a whole week to get it fixed did not impress me! However, the engineer set to work, pulling the machine out and then took great delight in showing me what the problem was. He held out what I thought was a plastic toy with four limbs outstretched. It wasn't a toy, though – it was a frog that had managed to get into the out pipe! How, I wondered? The answer was simple. The cat (who used to be called Jeremy, but is now known as BC – Bloody Cat) had brought the frog in through the cat flap and it had tried to get away. What a dreadful death for the poor thing! Whoever thought of cat flaps ought to be severely punished. BC has brought in (apart from several frogs) various birds, half a squirrel, mice (even bringing one into the bedroom at 4 one morning), all in various states of health, death and decay! I love him really, but I am rather pleased to have moved to a house with no cat flap.

Maxine Smale

New home, new name

Our cat arrived in our front garden about 13 years ago. I opened the front door and this small ginger and white fluffy bundle jumped straight into my arms. He had wandered far from home, crossing a busy main road to come to our house. He obviously knew where his real home and happiness lay. I did trace his original owners, but they were quite happy for me to keep him. His original name was Whisky, not a good name for a majestic ginger and white moggie, so we rechristened him Bombazine, a.k.a. Bomber, and sometimes The Flapmaster, when he proudly manages to negotiate his way through the cat flap. He loves warm, sunny days when he suns himself on our patio, next to his friend (made of stone), the lop-eared rabbit. He prefers company when he eats and my husband Alan often finds himself standing next to him in the kitchen at 5 a.m. while Bomber has a bite or two. What is it about cats that we allow them to wrap themselves around our hearts so completely!

Erica Potter

Double take

One day we found our elderly fluffy ginger cat keeled over dead in the garden, we think probably from a coronary. He was buried with due ceremony in the animal cemetery at the bottom of the garden.

Much later that night, our daughter was driving home, returning from her night's courting, when she accidentally hit a suicidal cat hurtling across the bypass. Unsure if the poor thing was dead or not, she put him in the boot and brought him home. She carefully placed the large fluffy ginger moggie on some newspaper in front of the lounge fire with a saucer of milk in case he 'came round', and crept to bed without disturbing us. The next morning, imagine my husband's consternation at finding the very stiff ginger cat on the fireside rug! His very furrowed brow was a picture to behold as he wandered off, muttering, 'I'm sure I buried that cat!'

Eve Ninall

Stumpy

Some 60 years ago my parents had a cat called Smut, whose tail was less than one inch long and when she had kittens, one of the litter had a full tail. Smut obviously did not approve, because she chewed the tail down to a stump like her own! We kept the poor kitten, which was named Babe, and when she grew she had two passions in life. One was eating liquorice, which my brother and I could easily supply from liquorice whirls, which were very popular then, and we were also lucky enough to live in a sweet shop. Her other passion was licking anything made of leather, such as belts. Looking back, I now realise that Babe was idiosyncatic!

Peter Stevens

Old winos

Our cats are called Shiraz and Syrah and are brother and sister. They are very alike and most people can only tell them apart if they up-end them!

John Ledward-Hands

Get a name!

My daughter and her husband got two eight-week-old kittens recently and still haven't named them. They are sisters, one all black and the other dark tabby. We have all come up with innumerable suggestions, all of which have been rejected for various reasons, and we have now run out of ideas. The first suggestions were lovely ones such as Florence, Ebony, Tabitha and Prudence, but have now deteriorated to Sybil, Gladys, Doris and the like. The kittens don't seem to mind at all, answering to 'little black one' and 'little brown one', but it is so frustrating for us! To cap it all, my sister has just acquired two barn cats to live on her smallholding and she is calling them Cat One and Cat Two!

Colleen

Tom-cat call

It doesn't matter what you call a tom-cat in my area – it always gets shortened to yargerroffoutofityabastard or thatfluffythingfromnextdoorisshaggingthecatagain!

Dominic Lund-Conlon

The joke's on me

Our first cat was called Rummy. Then we acquired Pepsi and Cola, but we *were* running a pub at the time! About nine years ago my son went to work away from home and shared a house, so he thought he would get two kittens of his own. He brought home one beautiful ball of fluff which he named Abbey, and one beautiful black slinky kitten which he called Ultimate Warrior, as he is an American wrestling fan. Abbey turned out to be a male, but he doesn't know, so we still call him Abbey. The cats and son came back home about six months later, so now I have the embarrassing job of taking 'Wozzer' to the vet's – Ultimate Warrior Rigby – not funny.

Bea Rigby

Indoor facilities

Years ago my then-husband found a new interest in Bonsai. He had acquired some Bonsai seeds and decided to plant them in a small wooden seed box, in special soil. All was prepared and seeds duly placed with great care. They were then left to settle on the cooker top out of the way, as we thought. But then our Siamese cat Sasha had other ideas. On discovering what she thought was a smashing indoor loo, I found her merrily digging a few holes to try it out, which she did! Hubby went spare, to say the least, as there were seeds and soil everywhere, while I was trying to pacify all round. However, the hilarity of it was too much for me and laughter prevailed, much to my husband's disgust – so cat and myself were in the doghouse for some time.

Doreen Hughes

Only when I'm ready!

Upon our return from holiday last year, we noticed that our garden shed had become a residence for a large stray cat. Having a favourable view of cats, we took it upon ourselves to feed this fearsome creature who promptly decided this was a good idea and ate the food we placed in the shed for him. After a few months, I was determined to get him into the house; winter was coming and I wasn't sure how he would fare in the cold weather. One damp Saturday, I managed to get close to this hissing and spitting ball of fur, tempting him with pieces of chicken and calling, 'Here, kitty-kitty!' when wham! I had the ferocious beast tight in my arms. His growls subsided as I stroked the back of his neck and told him what a good kitty he was. At that moment, my husband walked out of the house, curious as to what I was up to. The cat took one look at him and decided to leave, sinking his teeth into my left hand as he made good his escape.

By nightfall, my hand had doubled in size with what I can only describe as extreme pain. Upon my visit to casualty the next morning for what I thought would be a good telling-off and a nasty tetanus jab, I was admitted immediately and hooked up to a drip containing very strong antibiotics for the next 72 hours!

I gave up trying to coax the cat into the house for a while

after that, just installing a heater in the shed for him. In February, I came home one day and took out his usual dishes to his sumptuous abode. To my surprise, this big cat came straight out of the cat flap (installed in the shed door for his convenience!) and headed straight for me. 'Oh, no,' I thought, 'this is going to hurt.' However, the big baby wrapped himself round my legs, purring and miaowing, so pleased to see me, so I picked him up and got a big kiss for my trouble! Each day I got closer and closer, braver and braver. It took time, but we persevered and now I have a big softie who lives in the house and has found my side of the bed. In honour of his former home, we christened him Shedric.

Sam Taylor

Calling a spade a spade

14 years ago my daughter found a tiny kitten in her street. It was lost and when my wife and I stopped the car, she gave me the kitten. I turned it over and said, 'God, it's got paws like shovels!' – and that was his name for the rest of his wonderful life with us. Because of his unusual name, everybody knew him.

Ernest Raffan

Hot stuff

Years ago I knew someone who had two cats, one ginger and one jet black, called Mustard and Coleman. Thank goodness they were known as Moo and Boo for short.

Esme Mackins

Berobed cat

Although we have never been out to get one, my wife Pam and I were never without cats for the first 30 years of married life.

They just appeared somehow. But of all the many was one outstanding character of whom we still talk fondly.

One Saturday in 1979, my son Peter, then aged nine, and I came across a young cat sitting at the corner of our street. I said, 'Hello, Pussy Willow,' and we continued on our way home. The stranger promptly followed us along the street, into the house and jumped onto Pam's lap. We had no idea where he came from and he made it obvious that he'd decided to settle in with us, our two sons and other two cats. So we held a naming conference. Prominent in the news at the time was the Iranian religious leader, Ayatollah Khomeini. The cat had a black body and head, with a glorious white chest and forelegs. We kicked a few names around, and then I said, 'He looks like the Ayatollah in his robes.' That was it – the cat was named Ayatollah. This was usually shortened to Tollah. He was a very aloof and arrogant cat. After declaring his intention that first evening by jumping on Pam's lap, he never favoured anyone else in that manner. If picked up he would growl like a dog until put down.

When we had some building work done, he would climb the ladders and patrol the scaffolding. Tony the builder dubbed him 'The Building Inspector'. Ayatollah also came for walks with us, following me with Patch, our dog, usually for about 500 yards to the cemetery and once he made it almost a mile to the market place.

Michael Draper

Dog or cat?

The first cat my father had was a ginger tom named Fred Dog. My father's explanation of this was that he called him Dog simply because he wasn't one! Fred and Dad met when a colleague had a cat with a litter that he was going to dispose of. To avoid their drowning, Dad took Fred and his siblings home and found homes for all but Fred. Here began a long relationship.

Boris Banana was another cat which my parents had. He apparently had a tail shaped like a banana and this inspired my parents' choice of name. Boris was a black tom and a keen birder. One of his favourite tricks was to get up close to someone's face and then suddenly nip their nose!

The third cat to live with my parents was named Chippie Freeta. 'Chippie' came from my mother who thought the cat looked like her boss at the time, who in turn reminded her of a chipmunk; 'Freeta', because she was advertised as 'Freeta good home'!

A farm cat which came to live with my parents was named Biggles. He earned his name because every time my parents returned him to the farmhouse, he would apparently 'fly' back round to our house faster than my parents could get back! These are just a few of the many, but all interesting characters.

Sally Askew

Blushing dad

When I was about six I was a stubborn little girl who just wanted a pussycat. Eventually, doting parents agreed and there arrived a tabby kitten with a decided curl in the tail. Innocently, we named her after this curl. It wasn't long, however (this being the 60s), that Dad refused to call her in at night. It took some years before I understood how hard it must have been for a man to stand on a doorstep at night, shouting, 'Kinky'!

Liz Chapman

Caterwauling

We used to have a cat called Bananarama, so called by my husband because he said that when he trod on her tail, she'd squeal like the pop group of the same name! I just called her Rama for short. I couldn't get used to calling, 'Bananarama, dinnertime,' without dying of embarrassment.

Tracey Murray

Apt pairs

My brother's family had two cats named Biscuits and Crumbs. Another cat, called Feather, is 19 years old and seems to be going on for ever. Last year my niece was given a new kitten as a possible replacement for Feather. She called it Duster!

Jemma Jenks

Powers of persuasion

My gorgeous cat spent two very wet weeks during early January 1991, trying to convince me that I needed her. I spent those two weeks shouting through the patio doors, 'Go away – I am *not* a cat person!' But one particular wet night, I could stand it no longer, so I let her in. She had been out there most of the day getting wetter and wetter so, sitting on my kitchen floor, she got her name there and then. Everywhere she sat or walked she made puddle after puddle, so Puddle she became, a name which caused some smiles at the vet's. She was a beautiful cat with a lot of the Maine Coon about her. Judged to be about five when she chose me, she delighted me for a further 10 happy years, and certainly turned me into a cat person.

Christina Buxey

Day and night names

My cat thinks she is called Minky by day and Sodoff by night!

Janice Carter

Taken for a mug

Our first cat was called Pudden (short for Puddentat), because we couldn't think of anything else. Our second was all black with yellow eyes, so we called him Nick, as in Old Nick, although there was nothing devilish about him. A bit further down the line we acquired a very timid kitten, who nevertheless ate like a vacuum cleaner, so we called him Edgar, after J. Edgar Hoover. He is now quite fat, having a metabolic disorder, and so gets called Freddie (after Fredegar Bolger in *Lord of the Rings*) – also Eddie, Fatso, Podge and Splodge!

Finally, we acquired two sisters from a rescue centre. They were almost identical, black with white mittens, chest and whiskers. We couldn't tell them apart, so we put a red collar on one and a green collar on the other and called them Port and Starboard. Most of our cats have come from rescue centres, but the earlier ones just adopted us. I think we must have a sign in cat language at the bottom of our garden saying 'Mugs live here'!

Ann Baseden

Adventure cat

One of our cats is called Indiana and our surname is Jones!

Roger Jones

Also known as...

All of our cats have names, but they are mostly known by their nicknames. Kizzy is affectionately known as The Old Bag. She is very cute, but with baggy tendencies. Biddy is mostly known as The Dude, thick as two short planks, but a great gardening and mucking out supervisor. Dusty was inherited from my sister and is known as Dusty Bear or Bear Bear. She can read the kitchen clock and knows when it is 5 p.m. on the dot and thus time for tea!

Rachel Comley

Title?

We have a blue point Siamese proudly boasting the name of Awesome. He arrived in our household with a litter of kittens about ten years ago and, within a short time of being able to see and get about, quickly imposed his character on the rest of the litter and also upon us.

At the time, American football was becoming popular on TV and the most-used adjective by the commentators seemed to be 'awesome'. My young son David used to sit on the settee and provide commentary of the kittens playing and in no time at all it was evident that every move the blue point kitty made was indeed awesome! He is now an old gentleman, but still lives up to his name.

Tony Tickner

Singing cat

Recently my Mum was given a Persian kitten by some close friends. My first impression of it was 'When did it walk into a wall?' because of course they have very flat faces. After the months have passed, we have become great buddies and she sits on a cushion next to my computer. My Dad at the moment is very into the singer Dido, and as the cat is always singing, Mum decided to call her Diode!

Rebecca Howard-Carter

Cat raffle

We got both our cats from the Cats Protection League. When we picked them up, my wife Kathleen had a naming competition/raffle at work, with the winning names drawn from a hat. The proceeds went to the local Cats Protection League. The result of this competition was that the cats were to be called Buster and Codpiece (which was later changed by mutual consent to Codey). Some of the names that were suggested beggared belief: Lillette and Tampon, Laurel and Hardy, and Romeo and Juliet were just a few.

Ron Pethers

Hoity torty!

My wife and I had a beautiful tortoiseshell cat, which we called Shelley. She was of the common or garden variety, but she was so aloof at times, it was unbelievable; she would ignore you one minute, then smother you with affection the next. She lasted until she was 17 and we buried her in our garden by her favourite spot where she used to lie and sunbathe.

Ronnie Smith

Composed cats

My wife is a music teacher and our first two cats were called Felix (Mendelssohn) and Claude (De Pussy)!

Dave Pettit

No pips

Our 'altered' red tabby cat, who belongs to our son James is huge and goes by the name of Jaffa, because he is orange and seedless!

Gill and Andrew Charlton

Red cats

I used to live next door to a student of Russian political history who had two cats; one was called Trotsky and the other was called Mao (Miaow?).

Mick Warwicker

Long vacation

My sister Hazel had a cat called Wiggie, after Wiginald Bosencat (real name Reginald Bosanquet, the newsreader!) and he was a wonderful, extremely fat, black, white and ginger cat. When she moved house about 15 years ago, he went missing and she was devastated. Two years later, her new next-door neighbour knocked on her door to say that, knowing how much she loved cats, there was a fabulous looking cat sitting in her front garden in the bushes. Hazel came out to find Wiggie sitting there, looking at her as if to say, 'Where the bloody hell have *you* been?' Needless to say, she was over the moon, although absolutely amazed.

Barbara Lines

Flat cat

When we were first married over 30 years ago, the cat next door adopted us. They were a musical family and the cat was called B Flat!

Glen Woodward

Nutty names

My family is obviously beyond therapy with a mad collection of cat names. Our 14-year-old pair are called Romeo (as in Juliet) and Laser (as in the sailing dinghy), which teaches us not to allow children free rein with names which reflect their hobbies and interests. They also go on to develop warped ideas when they are old enough to have their own homes and menageries. Our eldest daughter has cats called Smelly and Bagpuss (for obvious reasons) – she also once had a guinea pig called Zaphod Beeblebrox! The middle daughter's cats are called Nicodemus and Spike (thanks to *Buffy the Vampire Slayer*); and the youngest has charge of Basil (who was once a pair with Sage). She also has a longing for three kittens and a puppy, so she can call them Athos, Porthos, Aramis and Dogtagnan! Is there any hope for us?

Chris Skidmore

Feline pairs

I have always adopted cats in pairs from the Cats Protection League, usually going for older males rather than kittens. Back in the 80s, we had two neutered toms called Marmi (after Marmaduke Hussey, the then BBC Controller), who was ginger; and Titus (full name Titus Andronicus), who was grey and white. In the 90s we took on Brian and Fred, so named because my husband was a Queen fan and thought Brian May and Freddie Mercury were great. Brian was black with white paws and Freddie was a long-haired white with a black tail. Uncannily, Fred had a kidney problem and died the same year as his namesake.

We now have a much younger cat who just turned up on our doorstep about four years ago and made himself at home – his name was already given – Tyson, and he can be quite vicious around your toes! We live next door to an elderly tom called Rambo, and he and Tyson can really make the fur fly!

Tina Jesson

Footie cat

I've had Crystal for 13 years. I got her from the Cats Protection League when she was just nine months old and my other cat, Rosco (named after Rosco P. Coltrane from *Dukes of Hazard*), was run over. She was a feral cat and I gradually got her to trust me, although it took five years. Her name was originally Chipper, but I changed it to Crystal because of my love for Crystal Palace Football Club.

Dave Bunting

Martial cats

I have two Siamese cats called Tai and Chi.

Jon Blackburn

Hat trick cat

My wife and I bought a kitten but didn't know what to call him. We are both Shrewsbury Town supporters and we attended a match where Gary Stevens played after injury and scored a hat trick. The following home match, Gary played again and the odds of him scoring another hat trick again so soon were enormous. So I said to my wife that if he did, we'd call the kitten Gary. Amazingly, Gary scored his second hat trick in two weeks, so we ended up with a kitten called Gary!

Bob Matthews

One-eyed waif

Several years ago during the school holidays, our children were staying on a farm and, while playing in one of the barns with their cousins, they discovered a tiny ball of fluff that had quite obviously been abandoned by its mother. It was very dirty and had one eye gummed up. Naturally, the children drew it to the attention of my sister-in-law, who pronounced it to be a boy and so the children had no choice but to call him Nelson. We adopted the tiny waif and took it to the vet, who said it was a girl – so Nelson became Nellie.

Jeremy Halliday

Midsummer Night's moggies

I have had a lot of cats, but sadly don't have one at the moment. One was called Cobweb, a delicate black and green-eyed creature, who would go mousing and come home with cobwebs on her whiskers. The funny thing is that when she was alive, we had mice in the cottage, but there hasn't been one since she went to the big hunting ground in the sky. She once presented us with a stoat and a baby rabbit, both alive and jiggling! Having also already had a Moth, my next cats will be Mustard-Seed and Pease-Blossom, so the *Midsummer Night's Dream* quartet will be complete.

Katie Lane

Flat escapee

An aunt in my family, who used to live on the top floor of a three-storey block of flats in south London in the early 60s, inherited a kitten. For the first week or so, the kitten was confined to quarters, to allow it to get used to living there. Everyone in the family was under strict instructions to make sure all points of exit were secure. But one day the kitten went missing, and the aunt went frantically in search of it. The flat was turned upside down, to no avail and nobody would own up to leaving the doors open. In despair and as a final resort, she went out on to the balcony of the flat and looked down to where all the local children were playing at ground-floor level, only to see the kitten walking furtively around amongst the cars and bikes. With no more ado, the aunt shouted out in desperation, 'Come here, sod ya!' From that day on, the cat's name was Sodya.

Peter and Susan Boorman

Vet fret

My late uncle, Terrance Tierney, had to make a visit to the vet with his long-haired grey cat, whose back end and legs looked enormous, as the poor cat had so much fur to contend with. My uncle, whose frame matched that of the cat's, was waiting his turn unsuspectingly, when the assistant called out at the top of her voice: 'Baggy Grey Pants Tierney, please!' My grey-suited, and now very red-faced uncle had to own up to who he was, much to the assistant's and everyone else's amusement.

Peter Rodgers

Fab friend

Twenty years ago we were adopted by Flump, short for flipping great lump! She was not much more than a kitten, with a huge hernia dragging on the ground, which had rubbed all the fur off. We took her to the vet, who operated successfully, and we brought her home. Two days later, she had to go through it all again, as her intestine was twisted. She made a complete recovery and became the craziest, most lovable and best friend in the world. She would tolerate the children's attentions, never scratching them and we accidentally trained her to come when we rattled keys. Her favourite game was hiding under a rug and batting our feet as we went by. We had an open fire and she used to lie in the hearth as close as possible to the heat, but amazingly never got more than the odd singe! Unfortunately, she got run over after about two years, but we still go all misty when we think of her.

James and Judith Stewart

Cat in straits

After we lost our cat at the ripe old age of 19, my daughter and son kept asking if we could have some kittens. This went on for some time, with the usual answer being, 'I expect so.' Eventually we succumbed to pressure and visited a cattery where Jodi and Ross both chose kittens. They were too young to take home at the time, so we had several more visits and then brought them home. When I asked Jodi what she was going to call her kitten, she immediately said, 'Spexo.' When we queried this, she explained that every time she asked us if she could have a kitten, the answer was always 'Spect so'! As for his brother, after a few days Ross decided to call him Knoffi (after Mark Knopfler) because he always seemed to be in Dire Straits!

Barbara and Derek Etherton

Pop cats

We went to collect a rescued six-month-old cat from our local sanctuary. He was originally rescued with his brother and they had been called Ronnie and Reggie. But when I saw him I knew just the right name for him. He was all black, beautiful, had the most wonderful voice and greatly enjoyed using it – so I called him Barry, after Barry White. He continues to use his wonderful voice to this day. His companion came to us a little later, via the possibility of being drowned in a bucket of water. He is another kettle of fish – ginger, beautiful, slick and with a swagger to his walk, he had to be Brian, after Brian Ferry!

Jeanette Anderson

Rude names!

Our cat Zoë is a Maine Coon plus something else and answers to a variety of names, including: Lush, Tart, Hussy, Ratbag, Slut, Cooking Fat, Tas (thick and stupid) and also Cheap-for-a-belly-rub – which she got from flashing to the local tom-cat! She is now 18 years old, has just had her thyroid gland removed and all her teeth, but we love her to bits!

Keith Reynolds

The Animal Health Trust

Feline Unit

The Animal Health Trust is a registered charity which aims to provide the science behind animal welfare. It achieves this by studying the diseases that affect companion animals and developing better methods of diagnosis, treatment, control and prevention.

The Trust has had a long-standing interest in feline diseases and, in recognition of the increasing importance of cats as companion animals, it is developing a new feline internal medicine referral service within its small animal hospital. There are now more cats (approximately nine million) owned as pets in the UK than any other companion animal.

The new 'Feline Unit' will thus be a fully equipped referral service dedicated to promoting feline welfare. The emphasis will be on individual, personal care of feline patients. Communication with clients and referring veterinarians will be a priority, and the ultimate goal will be to provide the best possible quality of veterinary care for cats.

Via the veterinary profession, the Feline Unit will provide a vital clinical service to individual cats and their owners. However, the Trust is equally concerned with broader aspects of feline health and welfare that can impact on the quality of life of all cats. These issues are being addressed by an internationally renowned team of scientists undertaking research into many important feline diseases.

The main benefits of the new unit will be:

- A staff of qualified nurses to provide complete 24-hour care for all hospitalised animals

- A comprehensive intensive care unit for critically ill animals
- A special unit to treat hyperthyroidism, which is a common condition, particularly of older cats
- A range of endoscopic instruments to allow non-invasive investigation of various disorders including gastrointestinal and respiratory problems
- Unique diagnostic imaging techniques including a highly sophisticated MRI scanner and state-of-the-art ultrasound scanning equipment

The Trust is already involved in epidemiological studies of feline infectious respiratory disease (cat flu). This is an extremely common infection and the studies will help to define risk factors associated with infection and optimal conditions and strategies necessary to prevent cats becoming infected. The Trust also has an active interest in feline hypertension. Just like people, cats can suffer from high blood pressure which can have devastating consequences on the cat, including the development of eye disease, which can ultimately lead to blindness. The Trust has been the major centre in the UK looking into the ocular manifestations of hypertension in the cat and how best to treat this condition.

With the development of the Feline Unit, further studies are being planned. A major area of interest is feline lymphoma (a type of malignant tumour which is particularly common in cats). These tumours are potentially treatable (with chemotherapy, surgery or radiotherapy) but there are still large gaps in our understanding of the condition in cats. The proposed epidemiological and pathological studies should help to identify criteria that will allow better prediction of response to therapy and thus prognosis for individual cats.

Chronic lower respiratory tract disease (chronic bronchitis or 'asthma') is also a very common disease of cats. The Trust has built up considerable expertise in the investigation of inflammatory airway disease in horses and it aims to apply this knowledge for the benefit of cats. Optimum therapy depends on a knowledge of the underlying disease process and improved methods of diagnosis are being sought which will allow the most appropriate therapy to be provided.

Trust scientists are also applying their expertise in canine and equine genetics to the study of feline genetics, with particular emphasis on inherited diseases. In time, the results of this, and other research work, will doubtless help in the treatment and welfare of cats seen by veterinary surgeons throughout the United Kingdom and beyond.

Animal *Health* Trust
the science behind animal welfare

Patron: Her Majesty The Queen
President: HRH The Princess Royal